# PRAISE FOR *MEANING MAKING*

"Chris Field has a gift for celebrating the overlooked ordinary and making every day an opportunity for extraordinary."

—**Mel Robbins,** *New York Times* bestselling author of *The Five-Second Rule* and host of the award-winning *Mel Robbins Podcast*

"There is wisdom in living an authentic life. We fear that being authentic might create conflict or limit opportunities . . . but when put into practice, it is liberating and brings truly meaningful human connections. That is what our world needs today, so I deeply value Chris's courage and vulnerability to share reflections of his journey to date. Chris's assertion that we are not broken is reassuring to all of us who have had similar thoughts and observations. I am eager to see what wisdom Chris draws from the world in the next phase of his life!"

—**Mark Roenigk,** head of hardware engineering at Facebook, former technology advisor to Bill and Melinda Gates Foundation, and director of Taelor's House Foundation

"Chris has done it again. He has written an amazing book full of stories and analogies that make reading it pleasurable and relatable. And more importantly, I personally identify with so many lessons learned. He addresses hard topics with such grace—what an enriching way to spend an afternoon. My head and heart are full."

—**Terri Dorsey,** former director of executive development, Boys & Girls Clubs of America

"Chris Field is an astute observer of the human condition. His purpose in writing this introspective book is to share his own life struggles in the hope that his experiences will help others make sense of their own. He has chosen vignettes that are, at once, both deeply personal and universally relatable. *Meaning Making* consists of many bite-size morsels that, taken together, constitute a veritable feast of valuable, hard-earned wisdom. Chris's optimism is infectious, and he makes a compelling case for the timeless value of believing that each of us is worthy of being known."

—**Dr. David N. McMurray,** Regents professor emeritus, former Peace Corps volunteer (Kenya), and former consultant to the World Health Organization

# MEANING MAKING

amplify
an imprint of Amplify Publishing Group
www.amplifypublishinggroup.com

*Meaning Making: Learning to Be Human Halfway through Life*



**For more information, please contact:**
Amplify Publishing, an imprint of Amplify Publishing Group
620 Herndon Parkway, Suite 220
Herndon, VA 20170
info@amplifypublishing.com

**Library of Congress Control Number:** 2024904059

CPSIA Code: PRV0324A

ISBN-13: 979-8-89138-077-6

Printed in the United States

To Stacey. Your grace and patience and love toward me feel unending. Or at least twenty-four years long (and counting). Thank you for helping me feel safe, even when I didn't know how to ask for it.

To my precious children. You are so much of my motivation to write and wrestle and do the work. So that you can be healthier than me. So that you can say we grew and learned together.

To my therapists. Both the licensed ones and the dear friends who have sat patiently and listened as I verbally started the process of working many of these topics out over the last couple of years. You know who you are (dear saints). If cell phone companies still charged by the minute, I'd owe you all a lot of money.

In honor of Uncle Curt. Larger than life, ever bold, and never without something to say. You lived big and inspire me not to take a single day for granted. Until we meet again, Chief.

# MEANING MAKING

*learning to be*

**HUMAN**

*halfway through life*

CHRIS FIELD

amplify
an imprint of Amplify Publishing Group

# CONTENTS

## PART 2: I AM WORTHY OF BEING KNOWN

## PART 3: I EMBRACE BEAUTIFUL MESSINESS

# NOTE FROM THE AUTHOR

This book goes against most conventional wisdom about writing a book. It doesn't fit neatly into a category. It's neither a memoir nor a self-help book. And it is starkly different from my previous books.

This book is based on a single promise: to bring myself fully to these pages in the hope that these stories might help you find more meaning in your life. Most everyone I know is hungry for more meaning, for something both bigger and beyond us but also something close enough to grab on to and hold. Maybe this offering will be that for you.

More than ever before, I have written authentically about hard and messy topics. These reflections are vulnerable and heartfelt—no pat answers or tied-up boxes or five-step action plans. They show how I am learning, growing, and stumbling through my own attempt to live out these truths: *I am not broken. I am worthy of being known. I embrace the world's beautiful messiness.*

The following pages are filled with the words and stories my own heart needed in this season of life, and now I want to share them with you. The goal of this book is not to sell a certain number of copies or get on prestigious bestseller lists but to make everyone who picks it up feel something. If I accomplish that for only a dozen people, then this will be a success.

Thank you for giving it a chance.

# INTRODUCTION

I watched in awe as Stacey's belly expanded with new life. My wife's body was nurturing a literal miracle, and I was excited to play my part. While she knit together bones and sinews, I began weaving together hopes and dreams. Each night, I would lay my head on my wife's stomach and tell my daughter that she was beautiful, that God made her, and that she was going to change the world.

Together we dreamed that our daughter would grow to be a woman of justice and mercy. When she was born, we named her Micah, after the great prophet and his memorable words about acting justly and loving mercy. And I continued speaking those words of life over her, praying for her before she could even fold her own hands.

Micah found her voice sooner than I had anticipated. By eighteen months, she was speaking in full sentences. I was amazed at the new words she discovered and the creative ways she used them. Suddenly, I had to watch what I said, knowing that she would try to repeat every phrase. My little girl was so confident and smart.

But something would shift when it was time to go to bed. Every parent knows the dreaded transformation that occurs at bedtime. Kids who hate to read beg for "one more story." Children who refuse to drink water are desperate for "one more sip." And if all else fails, the wisest of our offspring will sweetly request "just one more hug, Daddy."

Like many young children, Micah didn't want to be left alone in the dark. Or maybe she didn't want to be left alone at all. I wanted to protect her from anything bad or threatening or scary. But what could I do when the fear was all in her head? No amount of logic and no nightlights or alarm systems would assure her.

What would soothe her mind? What's the last thing she should think about before she'd fall asleep? What's the truest thing I could tell her? I tried "Mom and I love you," "We're going to take care of you," and "We're going to have a lot of fun tomorrow." None of that carried the weight I was hoping it would.

My words couldn't change how my daughter felt on the inside. Nothing I spoke over her affected what was going on within her. Never one to back down from a challenge, I began wondering if I could teach her an inward truth. Could I plant an idea in her mind, something so strong and good and true that she would return to it again and again throughout her life? Something to hold on to when the world seemed to be opening up and trying to swallow her whole.

"I am beautiful. God made me. I am going to change the world." These became Micah's words. Each night we would tuck her in, pray over her, and then prompt her to say her words. This became our rhythm, our routine, our nightly liturgy. By the time she leaves our house at eighteen years old, she will have said these words more than five thousand times.

Now she has something to hold on to when the world becomes scary and confusing. She can comfort herself when I'm not there. These words have truly become her words. They are part of her. She can recall them without hesitation, like an old scratch on the dining room table that's been traced with a finger thousands of times without thinking about it.

There will come a time when she questions these truths about herself. The middle school years find us all eventually. Someone may tell her she is ugly and broken, incapable and unworthy. Long before she faces those battles, I've taught her how to fight them. She has learned where the lifejacket is before she'll ever feel the fear of waves crashing over the sides of the boat.

Words matter. Rhythms matter. And they can change. Just like us.

My world expanded as my daughter grew. Eventually, Stacey and I added three more children to our family. I launched a nonprofit to eradicate child slavery in Ghana, published two books, and became a sought-after public speaker. I was changing the world and empowering others to do the same.

But the problem with trying to change the world is that the job is never done. The bar keeps getting higher and higher. Each achievement only illuminates the next one we must tackle. As a bullheaded person with a Type A personality, this drove me to work harder. There was always more to do, more to be, more to change. It exhilarated me, but others found it exhausting.

Some people heard my speeches and read my books and were inspired to run longer distances, climb bigger mountains, set world records, and start global charities. And that was exciting. But there was this whole other group of people who listened to me and walked away feeling defeated. They heard my story and thought, *There's no way I can do what he's asking. That's just not me.* My inspirational words were like a weight around their neck, making them feel weak, limited, and incapable. The exact opposite of how I wanted them to feel.

And still each evening, I went home and listened to my children proclaim, "I am beautiful. God made me. I am going to change the world."

At some point, I found myself with new questions I had never considered before: What if my child struggles with depression and needs to know that just making it to another day is a massive win? What if they face disease or disruption or disorder and feel guilty for focusing on their own healing? What if the words I gave them to cling to only end up dragging them down? What if my drive inadvertently cripples theirs? What if I was asking them to be like me instead of teaching them that who they are is more than enough?

I didn't want to be a father who added external pressure. Instead, I wanted to build my children up from the inside out. I wanted them to know, deep down in their bones, that they are good and worthy and valued not for what they do but for who they are.

My real hope wasn't that my children would change the world but that they would have the courage to show up as their true selves in the world. It's not flashy. It won't win awards. But it is vital. I know because I haven't always done it.

If I was going to teach my children to live authentically, I would have to lead by example. Somehow, I was nearly forty years old and still wondering, *Who am I?* Clearly, I had some work to do. So I started therapy. I dug deep. I got uncomfortable. And I began changing my own world from the inside out. Asking myself questions I never dared to ask before. Giving answers I never dared to admit before.

As I've evolved, so has my parenting. It is no longer good enough for my children to proclaim, "I am beautiful. God made me. I am going to change the world." These are good sentiments, but they aren't the most important truths I want to impart. So, I am rewriting these words, one by one.

Instead of "I am beautiful," may they proclaim, "I am not broken."

They will be bombarded with mixed messages about beauty throughout their lives. Models in commercials and airbrushed images in magazines will show them impossible beauty standards. Advertisers will try to convince my children that they are broken to sell them creams and clothes and convertibles to make them whole again. I want them to be able to roar back, "I am not broken."

The actual Oxford definition of broken is "fractured or damaged and no longer in one piece or in working order." Another meaning is "a person who has given up all hope." I want my children to know that even if they struggle or need to improve areas of their lives, the very fact that they wake up every day and keep trying means that they are not broken. They are very much in working order. Needing redemption or improvement is part of being human, not an indication that they are broken. My children are good and worthy and whole just as they are. Whatever they are is enough. I want them to embrace their story and view their limitations not as a curse but as a precious part of themselves. They are not broken.

Once we realize that we are not broken, our next task is to engage the world with that confidence. It's one thing to look in the mirror and accept ourselves; it's another thing to display that authenticity in front of other people.

We deserve to be known in our marriages, working relationships, and friendships. We need people who allow us to show up as our real selves and even demand that we do so. We should all have people in our lives who press us to push past our surface-level responses and who won't allow us to hide how we really feel.

I want that for me, for you, and for my children. May we all be able to say, "I am not broken. I am worthy of being known."

When we live from that place of authenticity and worthiness, it changes everything. Suddenly, the world is not a problem to be solved but a gift to be embraced. When our eyes are less focused on finding our own flaws, we find a new willingness to see beauty in the mess around us. Instead of endlessly changing and fixing, we find the grace to accept, love, and embrace everyone we meet and every place we find ourselves.

And so, thirteen years after I gave Micah her original words, I want to replace them with a different version. For her. For me. And for you too.

*I am not broken. I am worthy of being known. I embrace the world's beautiful messiness.*

These can be our words if we will let them. I truly hope we will.

# PART 1

# I AM NOT BROKEN

As you read these reflections, may you know deep down in your bones that you are good just as you are. Your value is not tied to your actions or accomplishments. You matter. And all those challenges you face and imperfections you see in the mirror don't mean that you're broken. This is what it feels like to be human.

# EXTRAORDINARY

My friend Reverend Rhoda shattered stereotypes in the best possible way. Of course, being a female priest in our small Texas town already made her stand out. But more than that, she was lively, animated, and loved a crude joke almost as much as she adored wearing her red high heels. I never knew a priest could be so much fun.

I loved being around Rhoda. She had a way of putting me at ease and making me laugh. I also really trusted her insight and valued her opinions, so eventually I asked her to join the board of Mercy Project, the nonprofit I started to eradicate child slavery in Ghana. She was a true leader in our community and a voice of wisdom and joy in my life.

Then cancer came, and it hit fast. Rhoda was only in her early fifties, but her health deteriorated quickly. Before I could even wrap my mind around her being sick, she was already on in-home hospice care. Her family was very protective of her time and space—and rightly so—in those final weeks. So, after she grew too weak to keep texting me, I worried I would never get to see her again. Then one day I got a message that Rhoda wanted to see me. I dropped everything and immediately drove to her house.

When I got there, she was in a portable bed in her living room, gazing into the backyard. Another dear friend of hers was rubbing her feet—one of the few ways left to soothe her pain. I was touched that this sixty-something-year-old teacher wrangled preschoolers all morning and then went to rub Rhoda's feet in the afternoon. She kindly excused herself when I walked in.

Rhoda beckoned me over with a smile. The cancer had stolen so much, making her skin pale and her face gaunt, but she still had that unmistakable sparkle in her eye. She was weak but seemed eager to talk. There was no room for chit-chat or surface-level discussion. Neither of us cared about the weather or the latest sports upset. Instead, we dove into genuine, honest, and heartfelt discussion.

Several times during our conversation, she told me how much she loved Mercy Project and how sad she was that she couldn't continue watching it grow. I thanked her for her leadership in the organization and said how very much we would miss her. Soon enough, I was crying. She reached out to hold my hand, and we sat for a moment in silence.

I tried desperately to put my thoughts into words. This would likely be the last time we would speak. How could I fully articulate what she meant to me? Our connection felt far deeper than the amount of time we'd spent together. From the first time I met her, I felt like I had known her for decades. She was one of very few people in my life who actually saw *me*, not the facade I worked so hard to maintain. And now I was on the verge of losing her.

After what seemed like a long time, I simply said, "Thank you for loving me so well."

She pulled me in close. "Chris, you are an amazing human being," she said. "Mercy Project is wonderful, but I'm not talking about that right now. I'm talking about you. You are extraordinary." I still cry every time I think about the depth and power and holiness of that moment. Of how badly I needed to hear those words from her. Of how deeply they resonated with me then and the impact they still have when I remember them all these years later.

Rhoda died just twelve days later, but those words, and the genuine love behind them, have continued rippling through my life.

Rhoda affirmed who I was deep in my soul. She assured me that she loved me for *who I am* and not *what I do*. Because her love wasn't tied to my actions or accomplishments, it healed something inside of me—the part that always wondered if I was worthy, the part that always felt a little broken.

I have wasted so much time chasing achievements and seeking accolades to prove my worth. I have spent so much energy trying to hide my brokenness. But Rhoda didn't see me as unworthy or broken or in need of accomplishments to cover up what I lacked. She looked at me, at the very essence of who I am, and called me extraordinary.

Every single one of us brings unique perspective and energy and characteristics to the world. We are all extraordinary. Yet far too many of us walk around assuming we are broken. Rhoda taught me that the greatest antidote to the poison of believing we're broken is having people who remind us we are extraordinary and that we don't require any accomplishments to prove it.

What makes us extraordinary is our own willingness to show up and be who we are. We often don't count that as extraordinary. We often waste time and energy hunting for the next accolade to make us feel worthy, never imagining that we were enough all along.

Rhoda's words freed something deep in my soul, ushering in freedom and joy where there had once been fear and worry. Now, in her memory, I try to go forth and speak those words to as many people as I can, including you. You are an amazing human being. Right now, just as you are, with nothing to fix or change or explain. You are extraordinary.

# DELIGHTED IN

Most mornings I lace up my shoes, walk outside, and start running before the sun rises. Some days I go willingly. Other times I have to force myself out the door. But I return to this routine day after day because of how it shapes my body, mind, and soul.

Running helps me think more clearly. When my body speeds up, my mind slows down. And as my legs spin and my thoughts become more tranquil, I often find myself talking to God.

One morning, I told God that I felt far away. Goodness, love, and hope were like distant memories. I wanted to feel closer to God. To divine goodness. To feel shalom, a Hebrew word meaning peace or wholeness.

A smile formed on my lips as a memory filled my mind: when my children were little, they would wake up from their naps hungry to be held. They would run on their little toddler legs into whatever room I was in and crawl up on my lap to snuggle with me. I would hold them close as my heart overflowed with love for them.

Then a new image came to mind, something I had never seen before. It was me crawling into the arms of God. God was a perfectly plump, older African American woman. I knew she was God like I know my own children are mine. There could be no doubt or argument or confusion about it.

This was unexpected, to say the least. I had grown up imagining God in one very specific way. He was old, white, and male. Often pretty mad too. Scripture is full of images of God as Mother, but those were never covered in Sunday School. It's hard to make the mystery of God palatable for children's storybooks, so we've oversimplified the divine. But that trade-off has come at a cost.

The more we try to define the undefinable or control the uncontrollable, the farther we get from the truth. We've swapped ambiguity for certainty, but that certainty doesn't come from God. God never asked to be put into a box or understood in human constructs. Instead, God claimed, "I am who I am," an unapologetically ambiguous description for something beyond explanation.

In that moment on my run, I was reminded that God is so much bigger than I could ever imagine. No allegory, simile, metaphor, image, or pronoun could ever contain God. Our human languages simply cannot capture the divine. Even if that truth makes us uncomfortable.

But even more than imagining God as a gentle grandmother, what happened next forever changed me.

I watched God stroke my cheek, smile at me, and pull me close to her. And in her smile, I could see that she was perfectly happy to be with me. My presence delighted her and made her feel real joy. She loved me completely, without reservations, demands, or restrictions. I didn't have to say the right thing or be a certain someone. I didn't have to give evidence. I was delighted in—just for being me.

I started to relax. I let go of my to-do lists, my important projects, and my never-ending quests to better myself and the world around me. In that moment, I was enough just as I was. Hard stop. I was loved, just as I am, and that was more than enough. In her joy, I found joy. As she loved me, I learned to love me. I began to feel as delighted with myself as she felt.

We all deserve to feel delighted in, yet so few of us ever experience it. We may be praised for doing the right thing, getting a good grade, paying off a debt, or checking any number of culturally acceptable boxes, but praise for *doing something* isn't the same as delight for *being someone*. It's a rare thing to feel delighted in for nothing other than being who we are. Many of us have never felt that way a single time in our lives.

You are worthy of being delighted in, with no disclaimers or asterisks or conditions.

That was the message this plump, Black, female God came to tell me.

After I shared this experience on my Facebook page, my feed devolved into a heated argument about gender, pronouns, and other political talking points. People could not get past the image of God as a woman. They missed the whole point of the story. It wasn't a theological statement about gender; it was a story of nearness and tenderness, of vulnerability and learning to be loved.

How often do we ignore God's great delight in us and miss invitations to be loved for who we are? How often do we choose to obsess and argue rather than to rest and be held?

I wonder what would happen if we spent less time trying to explain God and more time being held by God. As we experience God's delight in us, we might begin to delight more in others. And all the love God lavishes upon us might begin to spill out to the world around us.

As for me, I think I'm going to sit with her and feel loved like that, again and again, for as long as I can recall the lovely image from that surprising morning run.

# IMPOSTER MANIFESTO

No one has any idea what they're doing. Let's acknowledge that right now. Everyone is waiting for the real adults to step up. The bad news is that *we* are the real adults. We're the solution to the problems we're waiting for someone else to solve. No one is coming to save us, and no one has all the answers. That may feel terrifying, but it also gives us permission to finally, actually, really chill out. Realizing that everyone else feels as uncomfortable as we do is incredibly freeing.

We may be lost, but at least we're not alone. Everybody is a little bit lost and confused. It's like we're all walking around in a house that we've never been in before, and we've all got blindfolds on. Now there probably is someone in the corner of the house speaking confidently about the two square feet that they've been circling for years. They may call themselves a guru (first red flag) and act like they're one of the rare, special people who have it all figured out. But the truth is that they still have their blindfolds on, and they still have no idea what's happening anywhere else in the house. Just like the rest of us.

And no one, not even the most impressive "guru," has any idea what will happen next. I've talked with many successful business people, doctors, politicians, and leaders. No matter how much experience they have in the past, they still cannot predict the future. Every one of them shares that same feeling of insecurity and uncertainty as they move forward. Just like the rest of us.

They're not sure what will happen next because no one is sure what will happen next! Even a brain surgeon who has done 1,000 surgeries doesn't know exactly what they'll uncover on brain number 1,001. There's always some element of the unknown, unexpected, or unforeseen lurking in everything that we do.

Facing the unknown can be uncomfortable and frustrating. We like to imagine that our experience will insulate us from that pain even though we know it's not true. Our experiences prepare us for what happens next, but not perfectly. There's always some element of scrambling to figure it out. No matter how well we did in high school, college can still be a struggle. No matter how much fun we had dating, marriage is still a learning curve. No matter how easy the first child was, parenting two kids is still tough.

We don't know what we don't know until we face the unknown. And every time we think we understand our world or have grasped what's required of us, the world tilts and the rules change. That's why we all feel like imposters. Experience prepares us. Books prepare us. Education prepares us. But nothing can fully protect us from feeling like an imposter.

If you feel like an imposter, you should be proud of yourself because it means that you have some self-awareness. People who don't feel like imposters tend to be narcissistic jerks. And I think that deep down, they fear the unknown too. They just speak so loudly and with so much swagger and certainty that they fool even themselves into believing their own lies. I know this because there have been seasons of my life when I did this.

Imposter syndrome is not about being worried or concerned or fearful. It's about being a human being who wants to know what's next but can't. It's about realizing that no one in the history of the world has ever known exactly what tomorrow is going to bring. It's about feeling like you don't know what's going on because you *don't* know what's going on. And the imposter manifesto is about learning to name that, embrace it, be okay with it, and not let insecurities hold us back from moving forward.

The only time that imposter syndrome becomes problematic is when we use it as an excuse to shrink into the corner. Not knowing every answer doesn't mean we don't know some answers. Not being able to play every song on the piano doesn't mean we shouldn't play the ones we know. Not being able to hit the high notes doesn't mean we should stop singing. Every one of us has unique and beautiful gifts to offer the world. And we're called to share them, no matter how impostery (yes, I made that word up) we feel.

So if you feel like you're an imposter, congratulations! You're human. Welcome to the club. I'm glad you're here.

# TWO SIDES OF THE SAME COIN

I remember exactly where I was when my friend, Ken Fugle, made a life-changing observation. We were on a run together and having a difficult conversation about character traits and personality. Then he said, "Someone's best and worst qualities are two sides of the same coin. What makes someone great is probably also the same characteristic that will cause them the most pain in their life." I've been chewing on those words for ten years now, and they're not done with me yet.

Ken's wise words have definitely been true for me. Confidence is one of my best qualities. My confidence prompted me to start a nonprofit to help rescue children from human trafficking in a country five thousand miles away, with no money or wealthy friends. My confidence compelled me to run for mayor of my hometown at the age of nineteen. My confidence drove me to start a local marathon even though I had only ever managed one small 5K. None of those things would have happened if I didn't have confidence.

The other side of the coin is that my confidence can come off as arrogance. And when my extreme confidence *has* turned into arrogance, it has sometimes led me to hurt people. In my book *A Billion Hours of Good*, I shared a story about a previous employee of mine who told a mutual friend that I acted like I could do their job better than them. Ouch. It's been years now, and those words still hurt.

I haven't always handled constructive criticism well. That is mostly because I really want to please people and want everyone to like me. So those comments crushed me. Even now, many years later, it hurts to know that I made people feel that way. And since two people told me nearly the same thing, I wonder how many more employees felt belittled but didn't say anything.

If my confidence and arrogance are two sides of the same coin, then my task is to learn how to balance them. I don't want to be a bull in a china shop, throwing my confidence around to the detriment of those around me. But I also don't want to dampen my confidence because I'm afraid of offending people. I've been told since I was a little boy that I'm "too much," but it is equally dangerous to be too little. I don't want to fall into either extreme.

Instead of feeling broken by our negative side, we can learn to leverage it with our positive side. This kind of inner work requires a high level of commitment, self-reflection, and emotional maturity. We will need people to help us along the way. The key is finding the right people.

Some people always experience my confidence as a positive thing. They make me feel special and play an important part in my life. I feel loved and cheered on by them. I also realize that they're not the best judges of when my confidence has gone too far. So I can't take my cues from them.

On the other hand, I can list multiple people who always experience my confidence as arrogance. That may be due to their own insecurity, or perhaps they're too similar to me, or maybe I actually am acting arrogantly. Regardless of the reason, they feel annoyed or threatened by me. In their eyes, I am too overbearing, too intense, and too confident. I can't take my cues from them, either.

What I've learned is that I need to evaluate the source of a comment before I decide how to respond. People who only see one side of the coin are not very helpful. I can be grateful for the people who only see my good side, but I can't rely on their feedback. And I need to listen to the people who only see my bad side, but I can't try to shapeshift to meet their every demand.

We all need people in our lives who see both sides of us and love both sides of us. People who can evaluate us just as honestly when we are at our best as when we are at our worst. They are the brave souls who will tell us the truth either way. One trusted friend who loves me enough to tell me the truth is worth more than one thousand friends who will tell me what I want to hear. That's why I'm working to fill my life with people who can not only appreciate my confidence but also tell me plainly when it tilts toward arrogance. Because it does, and it will, and I need those people to call me out when it happens.

No matter how much I try to strike a balance between the two sides of my personality, I will never do it perfectly. And that's okay. Not in a "justify my bad behavior" sort of way, but rather an understanding that even these two-sided personality traits are part of what makes me human. So, if I can't have one without the other, then it's my job to learn to love and accept both, even as I work to amplify one and minimize the other. To learn to love and accept myself. All parts and sides of me. The good and the bad. The beautiful and the ugly. The confident and the arrogant, and all the other stuff that makes me, well, me.

# OUR SUPERPOWERS

Much of my life, others have told me that I am too much. I was a child with big dreams, big opinions, and a big personality. I wasn't trying to be too much. I was just being myself. I didn't want to be problematic or difficult or cause someone unnecessary angst. But I guess I did.

Now, at forty years old, I can draw a straight line from my "too-much-ness" to much of my success. A persistent child is annoying; a persistent adult is accomplished. An intense child is overwhelming; an intense adult is a strong leader. A stubborn child is frustrating; a stubborn adult is gritty. It turns out the very traits that made me obnoxious as a child have made me successful as an adult. They have become my superpowers.

I consider it a minor miracle that the intensity of my childhood survived into my adulthood. I'm grateful that all the things that made me too much didn't get completely squeezed out of me as I grew up. I've seen this happen to far too many people. They're born with an inherent sense of joy, an innate curiosity, and a tendency to embrace life with reckless abandon. But they're told that they're unrealistic or that they have to be responsible or that their dreams are too big. So they learn early to walk in a single-file line and look like everyone else.

Many well-intentioned adults try to squeeze children into shapes they were never meant to take. And all that training and molding only serves to squeeze the goodness right out of us, like Play-Doh overflowing the sides of a cookie cutter. So the child ends up in a socially acceptable shape, but they feel forever out of place, as though they don't quite fit in their own lives.

And what happens to all that goodness that gets squeezed out? Well, what happens to Play-Doh that's left out too long? It hardens. It gets stuck. It's beyond fixing. So when that child reaches adulthood and realizes that something is missing, it is really hard to regain what they've lost.

I think one of the biggest reasons that my too-much-ness didn't get squeezed out of me is that I received some positive reinforcement in young adulthood. When most people still thought I was too much, one woman saw my potential and praised me for it.

At the time, I was an eighteen-year-old camp counselor. It was the last day of a week-long camp for inner-city kids. A woman on the board of directors came to see the camp in action. As she approached, she heard my raspy voice yell, "Look out!" as a football sailed by her head. I had almost lost my voice from all the yelling, laughing, playing, and talking with kids all week. I'd been sharing my too-much-ness with them, and this woman saw how the kids were drawn to me. The following year, when I was just nineteen years old, that same woman helped convince her fellow board members to hire me as the director of the camp. When she told me this, I felt seen. Affirmed. And just the right size.

Many children are overwhelmed by the adults in their lives, and they don't get positive feedback in young adulthood either.

At some point, they decide, *If that's what it means to be me, I don't want to be me anymore*. They get the message loud and clear: "Don't be like that!" "Don't be like you." "You are obnoxious." "You are too much." They are like treasures who are told they have no value.

That's tragic.

As a parent, I have a kid or two who can be absolutely too much. I feel like my most important job is to parent them in a way that honors who they are. So I'm learning the balance between asking them to do the right thing and not squeezing out what makes them who they are.

This has made me empathetic to the adults who had to deal with me as a child. But I'm committed to not repeating their mistakes. When other adults mention something negative about their kids or mine, I'm quick to point out that I was once a little boy who was too much for the adults in my life, and it seems to have turned out okay for me.

When children paint and draw and color, we don't scoff at them. We don't expect their artwork to be as good as an adult's. We would never demean them for the skills they lack or tell them they are wasting their time. Instead, we let them mature. We let their gifts grow. We wait to see what will unfold. That's what I want to do with my kids' superpowers.

Each of us either feels like we're too much or knows someone who feels that way. Wouldn't it be beautiful if, instead of pointing out that intensity or passion or persistence with a huff and a sigh, we pointed out its spectacular potential? Wouldn't it be wonderful if we told children they are a gift to the world long before they feel like a gift to the world? Wouldn't it be amazing if no one ever felt like they were too much?

# STANDARDIZED TESTS

I've always said that when our kids got old enough to take standardized tests, we were going to throw them a big party. It would be called the "Ain't nobody got time to be defined by some test" party.

We would spend the whole evening talking about all the unique and beautiful ways God has gifted them that could never be measured by a test. We would fill the night with laughter and stories about how they're already using their lives and talents to make the world a better place. We would eat their favorite foods and talk about individuality and how people who march to a different drum are the ones who make the world go round (and usually have a lot of fun doing it).

We've also told them that when their scores came home, we would offer to throw them away without even looking at them. It's important to us that our children know their rank and performance don't define them. I want them to believe that they are enough, more than enough, just the way they are, and that no test score (good or bad) can change that.

Standardized testing marks the starting line of children being measured and known by how well they fit into a box. Before kids worry about what their peers are wearing, if they're listening to the right music, or if their parents' car looks cool in the pickup line, they take standardized tests. Before they face peer pressure, they face test pressure. I'm not sure which is worse.

The problem is that these tests push aside the broader genius of a child in order to measure "intelligence" in one very specific (but admittedly limited) way. It has been said that everybody is a genius, but if you judge a fish by its ability to climb a tree, it will live its whole life believing that it is stupid. The way we test our kids often seems to say, "If you do well on this test, you're a genius. If you don't, then you're stupid." Or at least that is what our children might hear if we're not intentional about doing everything in our power to offset that crushing messaging.

There is no way that a single test, discussion, or decision could ever define someone's value. A piece of paper can't measure a person's worth. Despite my strong feelings against these tests, I do understand why we use them. The world is messy and complicated. People are messy and complicated. So we try to reduce everything into manageable pieces that can be sorted and streamlined. But the things that make someone unique can't be measured in any course, degree, or job description. A human being cannot be defined by a résumé, a LinkedIn page, or a dating profile. We are all a nuanced, beautiful, messy mix of so many things.

This is what I'm trying to teach my children: They are beautiful, worthy, and delighted in, just as they are. A wrong answer on a test doesn't matter. Thinking differently from their peers doesn't matter. In fact, it's encouraged. I want my kids to know that the things that make them unique and set them apart are not bugs; they're features. It's all those things that make me love them so much. I don't endure their quirks; I adore their quirks. Their quirks make them who they are.

When Stacey and I threw our first "Ain't nobody got time to be defined by some test" party, it almost felt sacrilegious. Was it really okay to care so little about something we've been told is so important? Absolutely! That's why we keep throwing these parties year after year.

Over and over, we have found new ways to tell our children that we love them for who they are, quirks and all. We started a birthday tradition where we enjoy the birthday person's favorite meal and discuss two important topics: what we love about the person and what we hope for them in the next year. I believe those discussions are better gifts than any toys they receive. (I hope my kids will agree with me someday.)

We reinforce this lesson on Valentine's Day when we leave hearts on the breakfast table describing the five things we love most about each kid. I love standing back and looking at those twenty descriptions. They are all so different because each child is so different.

But there is one thing all of my children have in common. Not one of them has taken me up on the offer to throw away their standardized test results. I still ask them every time. How can I say the test doesn't define them but then rush to see their scores? That would be like telling my kid that all I care about is that they have fun playing baseball, and then yelling at them from the sidelines when they make a mistake. I don't want to raise hypocrites, so I'll try hard not to be one.

I believe deeply in education. I believe deeply in supporting teachers. But I don't believe in all the hype around standardized tests. They hurt our kids, and they hurt our teachers. A standardized test can't measure how a teacher makes a student feel. It won't show if a child feels safe in their classroom. No test could adequately measure the height and width and depth of love that teachers pour into their students every day.

So I think teachers should get a party, too. They need to be reminded that their ultimate success as a teacher is not in an arbitrary number but in teaching their kids about kindness and goodness and embracing the world's beautiful messiness. The same goes for parents.

Maybe we all need an "Ain't nobody got time to be defined by some test" party to celebrate who we are and lessen our obsession with what we do. Maybe the world would be a kinder place if we did.

# PARENTING

*Hey kids, if you're reading this, I really do love you. Feel free to skip to the next story until you're a parent too.*

I have great kids. They don't get into trouble at school. They get good grades. They're cast in leading roles in local theater productions, and they play on all-star teams. They check all the right boxes and have wonderful childhood résumés. Frankly, they're better kids than I was. I always loved the idea of being a parent. I grew up as someone who really wanted to be a dad. I wanted to have a big family. I love my kids dearly, I'm proud of them, and I know they're great kids. Still, parenting them is hard as hell sometimes.

I don't hear people talk enough about this. Instead, we brag about the medals they've won, post adorable photos on social media, or share charming anecdotes. And, of course, it's good to be proud of our kids and celebrate their successes. I do it too (see above). But it's equally important to tell the truth, that there were fifteen terrible photos before that one perfect shot and that sometimes, instead of bragging about my kids, I'm yelling at them. *Loudly.*

Maybe we don't tell the truth about how hard parenting is because we worry that we'll make our kids feel bad. I'm aware of that even as I write this. But our kids need to know it's not their fault that parenting is hard. They're good kids who are just trying to figure out childhood at the same time their parents are trying to figure out parenthood. It's happening at the same exact time. That's a recipe for trouble.

Parenting challenges my selfishness in ways I didn't even realize I was selfish. There are times when the last thing I want to do is be responsible for the emotional needs of four little humans. It's like parenting is a mirror that shows me all the things I didn't really want to see about myself. It stretches me to the very limits of what I think I can take and then asks for just a little bit more. Sometimes I have more to give. And sometimes I don't.

When I'm struggling to be patient or speak kindly or show up emotionally at the end of a long day, or lean in when I just want to completely detach, it would sure be nice to know I'm not the only one who feels this way.

There's no prize for the person who acts like everything is fine no matter how much pain they are in. We've all seen the meme of a dog with fifteen fires behind him, and he's just muttering "This is fine" as the world literally burns behind him. How many parents are going through life like that? We walk out of our homes where there are fifteen fires raging, and we tell everyone we're fine. If that's you, this is your sign that it's okay to not be okay. It's fine to say it's not fine. Parenting is real, and it is hard. Sometimes really hard.

If parenting is the hardest thing you've ever done, you're not alone. You are not the only one who struggles in this innately challenging role. Let's normalize acknowledging that parenting is incredibly beautiful and also incredibly hard. Both of those things can be true. And it can be true no matter what kind of person you are or what kinds of kids you have.

It is an extraordinary responsibility to be tasked with shaping a life. It's a huge, divine, beautiful responsibility. I like it, and it's hard. I enjoy my children, and it's hard. I love being a dad, and sometimes it's hard. And that's okay. The best stuff usually is.

# LONELINESS

Evidently, American men are lonelier than ever. I read a whole article on it the other day. But I didn't need those scary statistics to tell me this. I've lived it. I've known it. I've walked with the ache of loneliness. I'm guessing many of you have too.

There is plenty of research out there about the rise of loneliness and how it is damaging more and more people's lives. But I haven't seen many articles that explore why this is happening. Maybe some of the simplistic answers are that we're too busy, we're wasting time on social media, or we're under so much pressure to achieve and make money. But I don't think those reasons get to the root cause of the problem.

I think most men are lonely because we believe that we're broken. So we put up barriers and keep everything surface-level to prevent anyone from finding out. The deep-seated belief that there is something wrong with us prevents the deeper connections we crave. This inevitably leads to loneliness.

It's not that we don't talk to other men. We're having conversations. We're playing in softball leagues. We're going out for lunch with our colleagues. We're in the same spaces, but our relationships lack emotional depth due to a shared (but never *shared*) belief about ourselves that we're broken in some way.

We are "friends" on social media with more people than we've ever known before. I'm twenty-two years out of high school, and I could discover any of my old classmates' jobs in about five minutes, even though I have no present relationship with them. I can almost fool myself into thinking they're my long-time friends. But knowing something about a person is not the same as knowing the person. We've lost the distinction between those two things. We "know" hundreds of people, but we often don't really know anyone.

Of course, women also deal with some of these issues. So why aren't they as lonely as men are? I think it's because there is a cultural expectation that men should be confident and courageous. That might translate into more promotions at work, but it also correlates with more loneliness.

Men are often rewarded for having it all together. So we're scared to reveal the places where it's all falling apart. It's easier to talk about sports or the weather. We may broach the subject of money, but we couch it in the most comfortable way possible: "Everything has gotten so expensive. Oh, the price of college these days!" This allows us to show our concerns without making them personal. There is no risk in those conversations. You don't have to bring your whole self into them. You don't have to show your brokenness.

The belief that there is something broken about us makes us terrified to enter into deep relationships. We don't want anyone to know the "truth." It's like each of us is walking around with the same leg injury and pretending we're just fine. When we're around other people, we walk normally, no matter how much it hurts. Then when we're by ourselves, we immediately start limping again.

Everyone is hurting. Who is going to be the first one to name it? Hi, I'm Chris. I'm naming it. I need more depth. I need more real friends. I'm hurting. And I'm so tired of the shallow, held-back, not-quite-the-whole-truth chatter that fills so many of our lives and relationships.

I believe loneliness will continue to plague us until we can share openly, even about "taboo" topics like sex, money, and faith. You know, the big stuff that bothers us. We need to start having honest conversations about our deepest worries and fears—no matter how terrifying that is. Until we have a mutual exchange of vulnerability and acceptance, we'll just continue being lonely.

If we don't make changes, we'll just keep on talking about our new phones and how busy we are and the surface-level details of our lives. We'll keep having hundreds of shallow conversations a week. It's up to us to show up and share more.

This level of sharing comes with risk. I have some male friends who don't want to have this kind of relationship. I try to be vulnerable, and they refuse to return it. They feel safer in the shallow end and don't want to swim with me. There are some tricks you can only do in the deep end because they're too risky in shallow waters. So we'll forever be in a limited friendship. I don't think either of us is better for it, but it's beyond my power to change the dynamic.

It's uncomfortable to discover that a relationship isn't growing deeper. But it does free you up to continue looking for and eventually finding relationships where your depth is received, reciprocated, and returned. And that's the only true antidote for loneliness. For all of us.

# SHARED HUMANITY

I was in San Diego on a business trip, quickly realizing why people pay millions of dollars to live there. The sixty-degree weather was dreamy, much better than the sweltering heat I'd left behind in Texas. I was glad I had brought my running shoes.

Early one morning, I went for a run along the harbor. I passed the USS Midway and marveled at the huge naval warship. Next, I saw the Maritime Museum with its amazing historical vessels. And all along the way, I enjoyed beautiful blue water and stunning views.

The sounds of a woman crying startled me out of my blissful state. I glanced over my shoulder and realized that as the sun rose, the local homeless population did too. Dozens of tents and makeshift shelters were crowded together in various states of disrepair. Three policemen confronted a woman who stood outside her tent. She sobbed as they looked on.

I turned back to the ocean. It sparkled in the rising sun, unfazed by the suffering of humanity a few feet away. The contrast was jarring. We live in a world where beauty and pain constantly butt up against each other. It's hard to know how to respond.

In some seasons of my life, I would have expressed sympathy for the people living in tents. Then I would have soothed myself by subconsciously considering the myriad of ways we're not the same. If I focused on their shortcomings, then I could distance myself from their pain.

A little farther down the dock, I saw a man setting his crack pipe on a trash can, ready to forget he was homeless for a while. I kept running and thinking and trying to process all of the ugly, beautiful reality around me. Then I saw a man pulling all of his worldly possessions in a grocery cart. He was sweeping the public sidewalk. It struck me as so odd. Why did he carry that broom with him? Why was it important to him? A little farther down, a disheveled man sat on a park bench, cleaning his shoes. He was meticulous and focused, just like my thirteen-year-old daughter making sure her Nikes were shiny and white.

All in a five-mile run.

Life is more complex than we could ever imagine. We are more complex than we could ever imagine. And no matter how we may appear or how low life has beaten us down, none of us is broken. This is the truth we must accept about ourselves and share with others.

I am not broken. I've been learning to let go of the negative beliefs about myself, all the parts of me that I once called unworthy. If I'm going to do that for myself, then I also need to do that for everyone around me. Is it even possible to do it for myself if I can't do it for others?

The people I saw on my morning run didn't exactly look or act like me. They weren't in the same life position as me. But just like me, they weren't broken either. Yes, they were wounded, hurting, and down on their luck. Yes, they were low on hope and struggling to survive, but none of them were broken.

I wondered what they believed about themselves. How many times had they been told, in word or deed, they were broken?

How else could they interpret someone moving to the other side of the street to avoid them or staring straight ahead in their cars to ignore them? I wondered when they started to feel like they were broken. When was the first time someone had said it to them, and at what point did they hear it so much that they began to believe it?

# FLAWS

Do you want to find a seventy-year-old with chiseled abs? You can find it on social media. Do you want to find a ten-year-old graduating from college? You can find it on social media. Do you want to find someone doing something ridiculous that you had never even thought of before? Yup, you know where to find it.

Social media is like the Olympics: the best people in the world show off their talents on one stage. But instead of every four years across just a handful of specialized events, now every day is the Olympics, and there are infinite numbers of events. Social media provides a daily reminder of all the ways that we're not the best. And that stings. Even though there can literally only be one "best" in each category, we often feel bad that it's not us.

Seeing someone else's strengths makes us evaluate our weaknesses. We don't just think, *Wow, that's amazing for them.* We think, *Wow, what's wrong with me? Why can't I do that?* It's like other people's accomplishments are a giant spotlight revealing our lack of accomplishments. We can even see someone doing something that we never cared about before, and suddenly we feel bad that we can't compete.

Far too few of us are satisfied with ourselves, our lives, or our bodies. Social media feeds this dissatisfaction. It makes us think that maybe we'd be satisfied if we had what he has or looked like she looks. It keeps us in an unhealthy loop of obsessing over other people's accomplishments and hyperfocusing on our own flaws. We look at people's strengths and feel weak. We look at our weaknesses and bemoan other people's strengths. And on and on it goes. How could we not feel broken when this is the never-ending loop that plays on the little device in our hands every day?

The problem is that social media shows the good without the bad, the light without the shadow, the accomplishment without the collateral damage. If we saw the whole picture, we might feel very differently about the outcome.

What if each incredible accomplishment were paired with details about what that person gave up to be in that position? We would see a successful businessperson in a corporate jet and the broken family left behind. We would see a person with an extraordinary body but also the eight-hour gym days and terrible body image that drove them to it.

I'm not suggesting that we achieve excellence only through unhealthy means. I strive to live a life of excellence myself. I tell my kids all the time, "Greatness is a choice. A daily choice." However, I know that every time I say yes to investing my time and energy in one area, I'm also saying no to the countless other opportunities I could be pursuing. There is a cost to everything we choose.

When we see a perfect post on social media, we don't see the cost behind it. Social media doesn't show us our heroes' backstories. We just see people on pedestals who make our lives look boring in comparison. But if we knew the cost they incurred to get there, we might be more satisfied with what we have. If we saw their collateral damage, we might be a lot more grateful for the balance we've achieved. If we saw the whole picture, we might be a whole lot more content with where we are and what we have.

When we focus on our flaws and the perceived perfection of everyone else, we miss the incredible opportunity to love ourselves and others in all of our beautiful, messy complexity. We lose the chance to appreciate all the stuff that makes us who we are.

It reminds me of how women often view their post-pregnancy bodies. Of course, all of my knowledge is second-hand, but as the husband of a wife who's had four babies, I have seen what a struggle it is for women to reclaim their bodies after multiple pregnancies. They so often look at their bodies as worse than before they had their babies.

They lose sight of the fact that they grew an actual person. They took part in a literal miracle—they created a life! Their blood and muscle and tissues, the food they ate, and the water they drank created a human being who will one day walk around and solve real problems in the world. It's inconceivable (pun intended). But that's not what most women think about when they look at their post-pregnancy bodies. They only see the flaws.

It's such a tragedy that every woman who has ever given birth doesn't feel like the absolute Chuck-Norris-level ninja that she is but instead sees her post-pregnancy body as imperfect. And it's not just mothers. When the standard is airbrushed or video-edited perfection, we all have plenty of flaws, and we all have the capacity to obsess over them so much that we ignore the literal miracle of life in front of us and inside us.

# TRUE VULNERABILITY

Long ago, I was a seminary student studying Greek, the language of the New Testament. At the end of the first semester, right before we all left for Christmas break, my professor told me something I've never forgotten.

She said, "Don't go home and tell people everything you know about Greek. You know just enough to be dangerous. You don't yet know enough to add value to anyone's life, but you absolutely know enough to cause confusion and angst. Don't do that."

I've thought back to that statement many times over the years. It's dangerous to present ourselves as experts when we're really only novices. Unfortunately, I did a lot of that in the first half of my life when it came to vulnerability. I had a vision of myself as a powerful leader with a high emotional IQ and an innate gift for connecting with others. Playing that role required a level of vulnerability that I didn't possess. So I faked it.

I knew just enough about vulnerability to be dangerous. I could throw around the right buzzwords and fool people into thinking I was being vulnerable. But in reality, I was often just moving myself into a position to achieve whatever I was truly after. I know that sounds nefarious, but I truly thought I was being vulnerable. All of my angling and acting was done subconsciously.

It wasn't until I discovered what real, authentic vulnerability looks like that I realized how shallow my strategic vulnerability had been. Just like it's not until you finish your fourth semester of Greek that you realize how little you knew way back at the beginning (and how much there still is to learn).

When I took my first, cautious steps into real vulnerability, I was terrified. My strategic vulnerability had always kept me safe. It allowed me to hide the parts of myself that I found shameful or unworthy or broken. It felt risky to open up my perceived brokenness to someone else. What if they merely validated the terrible things I already thought about myself? What if they took my vulnerability and used it against me?

Then my therapist helped me realize that there wasn't something inherently wrong with me. I wasn't failing at life while everyone else was crushing it. We are all just muddling through the best we can. We all have stuff we struggle with. The fact that we have struggles doesn't make us broken; it makes us human. Once I realized that, I was much more inclined to at least try to start bringing my whole, vulnerable self into every relationship.

If we can accept the reality that every person we pass by or work with or wait in the parent pickup line with is dealing with their own struggles, it gives us the courage to share ours more openly. Everyone is going through life with the same trepidation, lack of confidence, and uncertainty. We all spend most of our internal lives like a little baby deer learning how to walk for the first time.

I've discovered that vulnerability isn't the weakness I feared it would be. It's actually a beautiful gift. One of the biggest blessings of vulnerability is that you end up articulating feelings other people have but don't know how to say or don't feel safe enough to say. Sometimes I post my insights on social media and people respond that they didn't know how to articulate their feelings on that topic until they read my words. There is no greater honor for me as a writer than for someone to say, "I didn't have the words, and you gave them to me." Helping others make meaning out of their own life and experiences is a gift, but it's impossible without some level of true vulnerability.

I'm desperate and committed for the second half of my life to be marked by more vulnerability. If the first half of my life was about parading around like a peacock, showing the world that I'm worthy (and fearing they'd see that I wasn't), I want the second half to be about uncovering what I previously worked so hard to hide. My reward will be the opportunity to make a deep connection with another human being.

Sometimes being vulnerable is clumsy. It's like I'm trying to fist-bump and the other person goes for the high five, or I'm ready for a hug and the other person tries to shake hands. That's how vulnerability feels sometimes because most of us have so little practice with it. But that just encourages me to keep trying. I long for a world where we laugh through those awkward moments together and don't let them deter us from leaning into vulnerability—true, nonstrategic, we're-all-in-this-mess-together vulnerability.

# PART 2

# I AM WORTHY OF BEING KNOWN

It took me a decade to learn these truths: *I can be vulnerable. I must be honest with myself. I need to let the real me show.* These are the stories of my becoming. May they accompany you on the painful, wonderful, often overwhelming but always worth it journey of revealing who you are to the world.

# BECOMING REAL

Almost two decades later, I can recall two crystal clear images of my wedding day: my beautiful, glowing bride and my not-so-beautiful, glowing bald spot. Yes, I started losing my hair at twenty-two years old.

Thankfully, I had no idea about it during the ceremony. But when we received the wedding video, filmed from the top of the balcony at the back of the church, I could no longer run from this surprising new truth. The video had captured my thinning scalp in all its glory. What a shock. What a shot to my pride. What a blessing to realize that Stacey had noticed for months (years?) and still loved me enough to pledge her whole life to me—hair or no hair.

There are many products and procedures to cure baldness. In my twenties, I didn't have the money for them. And by the time I hit my thirties, I didn't care about them anymore. Our culture views balding as a problem, but I no longer do. Losing my hair initially triggered deep insecurity but then ushered in even deeper love. Why would I want to hide that?

As Stacey and I enter middle age (a phrase that, like the Middle Ages, brings to mind thoughts of death and darkness), we're returning to this lesson in a new way. We find ourselves asking, "Are we comfortable in our own skin? Can we accept our wrinkles and embrace our gray hairs? How much time and energy and money will we invest in trying to pretend that we're still twenty-two? And why on earth are so many people around us so terrified of growing old?"

This line of questioning doesn't stop at our physical appearance. As "over the hill" parties loom on the horizon, all sorts of deeper questions are being stirred up: "Have we hit our peak? Do we even know who we are? Can we even remember what we like? Do we have any idea where we want to go from here?"

Just like I could find many solutions to balding, there are also many sources of wisdom for these midlife stirrings. The best one I've found came to me while I was mindlessly scrolling through my Facebook feed. I had read these words as a child, and they went right over my head. I had read them again as a teenager and thought they were stupid. When I returned to them as an adult, they made me pause. Or, more accurately, they punched me directly in the gut.

These simple words from a beloved children's story are like little daggers shooting holes in how we try to safely engage the world. They're an invitation, a dangerous one. If you read them with an open heart and mind, a veil will be lifted, and you'll see the world in a new way. You may be tempted to just skim through them and move on, as I was. But if you're willing to sit with them, they may just change everything.

*"Real isn't how you are made," said the Skin Horse. "It's a thing that happens to you. When a child loves you for a long, long time, not just to play with, but REALLY loves you, then you become Real."*

*"Does it hurt?" asked the Rabbit.*

*"Sometimes," said the Skin Horse, for he was always truthful. "When you are Real you don't mind being hurt."*

*"Does it happen all at once, like being wound up," he asked, "or bit by bit?"*

*"It doesn't happen all at once," said the Skin Horse. "You become. It takes a long time. That's why it doesn't often happen to people who break easily, or have sharp edges, or who have to be carefully kept. Generally, by the time you are Real, most of your hair has been loved off, and your eyes drop out and you get loose in the joints and very shabby. But these things don't matter at all, because once you are Real you can't be ugly, except to people who don't understand."*

—Margery Williams in *The Velveteen Rabbit*

No one aspires to be "loose in the joints and very shabby." It goes against everything we've been taught to value. Rather than loving the Velveteen Rabbit's Realness, we would much prefer the brand-new, untouched toy which has endured nothing, overcome nothing, felt nothing, experienced nothing, been nowhere, created no value, and birthed no joy. Our culture values the object that is still in the box more than one that has clearly experienced a life worth living and has the badges of honor to prove it. What a tragedy.

Our culture has such backward definitions of loveliness and beauty and value. If we buy into it, then we can enjoy about ten years of fitting the mold of acceptability before spending inordinate amounts of time and money fixing the ever-mounting signs of our wear and tear. In short, if we believe that new is better than Real, we will be forced to pretend we are still new and hide any evidence to the contrary. And we will spend our entire lives looking into the tiny rear-view mirror instead of looking at the good all around and still ahead of us.

This kind of pretending is a game we can never win. It will never be enough, no matter how many changes we make. We can twist and turn and put on every costume, wear every hat, do our hair in every different way (for those of us lucky enough to have any), and buy all the things to cover our flaws, hoping and praying that the people who will never understand us might finally accept us. But why?

The irony is that even if they did accept us, they wouldn't actually be accepting *us*. They'd be accepting a cartoon-character version of ourselves, one we can never fully maintain. And trying to keep ourselves in that false state is highly uncomfortable. It's like putting on a pair of jeans that are way too tight. We can barely button our pants, and now we have to sit through the rest of the meal. There's no way we can truly savor what's in front of us. I've been there. You probably have too. And you've probably found it's not worth it to keep pretending.

So what's the other option? What can we do once we decide we will no longer seek after the insincere, fleeting applause of others? Well, the alternative is just as terrifying, perhaps more so. Being vulnerable enough to be Real requires us to risk losing everything—all of our control, all of our outward signs of success, and all of our upper hands. It requires us to be Real about who we are deep inside, what we wrestle with, what keeps us up at night, and what we're scared to even admit to ourselves.

That's why reading this passage from *The Velveteen Rabbit* feels like looking at the sun. I immediately want to look away. It's uncomfortable, and I'm afraid of what it will reveal within me. It challenges something very deep inside me. Becoming Real feels dangerous. It would mean tearing down the guardrails I've put up to keep myself safe and slowing down long enough to share what's really going on with me. So although I want to sit with this passage, I also dread sitting with it.

I want to be loved for who I am, flaws and all. But I'm scared of the process of becoming Real and the rejection that may come from the people who don't understand. It's easier to remain on the surface where it's calm rather than sharing deeply and upsetting the status quo. But, just like that wedding video, this passage reveals a truth that I can't unsee, unknow, or unlearn: I haven't always been Real, though I desperately want to be. Because the only thing scarier than losing control and becoming Real is imagining spending my whole life hiding from myself.

# FEELING MY FEELINGS

Hi, my name is Chris, and I'm a people pleaser. If someone is nervous, I immediately try to make them more comfortable. If someone is lonely, I jump to assure them that they're valued and welcomed. If someone is confrontational, I go out of my way to explain that we all have shared goals. Basically, I try to read other people's feelings and help them handle their emotions.

So imagine my surprise when my therapist told me that I needed to learn to name my feelings. I almost rolled my eyes! I can name everyone else's feelings, so why in the world would she think I can't name my own? She may have suppressed an eye roll of her own when she replied, "Well, of course you can name everyone else's feelings because that keeps you safe. But your own feelings are much riskier to name." She had me there.

Understanding other people's emotions gives me a measure of control, but feeling my own feelings makes me vulnerable. It's much safer to be numb. Then nothing can hurt me. But the moment I start examining my feelings, things can get out of control pretty quickly. Other people's emotions are endlessly fascinating, but I had a gut feeling that mine couldn't be trusted.

At the end of our session, my therapist gave me an assignment: The next time I was in a room full of people, I should ask myself, "How do I feel right now? What do I want right now?" That's all I needed to focus on. I wasn't supposed to anxiously scan the room trying to understand other people's feelings. It was time for me to learn to examine my own.

A few days later, I went to an event at my daughter's school. Walking in the door, I could literally feel my "people-pleasing" lens click into place. I scanned the room and saw someone who had recently made a large donation to my nonprofit. I knew it would mean a lot to her if I went over for a chat. Plus, it could lead to more money to help more people. But no. That wasn't what tonight was about. I wanted to stay with my wife and daughter. So, I did.

For a few brief minutes, I was content chatting with my family. Then I saw a man who used to go to our church. There had been some drama when he left. A quick glance in his direction told me that he was feeling defensive and scared of being judged. I knew exactly what I could say to put him at ease. Plus, it could lead to a nice reconciliation story. But no. That wasn't what tonight was about. I wanted to stay with my wife and daughter. So, I did.

And on and on it went. The room was full of people to please, hands to shake, babies to kiss, egos to boost, and relationships to grow. I did none of that. Instead, I chatted with my beautiful wife, enjoyed meeting my daughter's friends, and felt my feelings. When we walked out the door after the event, I felt calm and content.

That evening revealed just how much energy I usually spend looking around rooms, trying to understand other people's feelings without ever examining my own. It makes about as much sense as playing poker without looking at my own hand. If I'm not capable of understanding my own feelings, it's pretty irresponsible to try to handle other people's feelings. That can fall into manipulative, controlling behavior pretty quickly.

I never meant to be manipulative or controlling. I thought my ability to read other people's emotions was like a superpower, and it can be a really valuable skill when used responsibly. The problem is that I couldn't always tell if I was responding to people's emotional needs for the right or wrong reasons. Did I want to be kind to the donor, or was I trying to push her to make another donation? Did I want to befriend the man who left the church, or was I trying to be the hero who mended a broken relationship? I had no idea. I just knew that I didn't want to be a people pleaser anymore.

The antidote to people pleasing is feeling your feelings. So that's what I'm learning to do. Of course, the problem with my feelings is that I don't get to choose them. There's no way to only experience the good ones and stay numb to all the bad ones. My only choice is whether to feel all or none of them. Pain, disappointment, sorrow—each of those terrible emotions might be lurking inside of me. There could be joy, gratitude, and peace, too. I just have to be brave enough to find out.

# THANKS FOR YOUR SPERM

Sex was a taboo topic when I was a kid. Our parents mostly avoided it. The church condemned it. And our teachers only spoke of it in scientific terms (like that one time, in that one middle school health class, with that one poor football coach who was stuck teaching sex ed).

My wife, Stacey, and I have taken a different approach. We talk about sex with our kids. Openly and often and from a very young age. We take on tough, complex, confusing, messy, nonlinear, and not-neatly-tied-up topics because we believe this will help our children grow into better adults. No matter how uncomfortable we feel along the way. Their growth is worth our discomfort.

If I want my kids to *think differently* about sex than I did at their age, then I'm going to need to *talk differently* about it. That means shame-free conversations. That means talking about sex around the dinner table. That means telling our kids that no question is off limits and promising that we'll always tell them the truth.

When I was growing up, most of the authority figures in my life were mostly silent about sex. So I learned all the wrong things, in all the wrong places, from all the wrong people. That's what we're trying to avoid. We want our kids to know that their parents know more about sex than their friends. We're the experts on this topic, so they should always come to us for answers.

This leads to conversations that force me to deal with my own fear-based, sin-laden conditioning about sex. When my middle schooler comes home and asks why people giggled in math class when the answer was "69," part of me wants to shut down the conversation as quickly as possible, but the other part of me knows that "comfort and growth can't ride the same horse." I have to be willing to be uncomfortable so my kids can grow beyond the terribly unhealthy and myopic perspective that sex is dirty or shameful or wrong. Because ten-, fifteen-, and twenty-year-olds who are subconsciously taught that sex is bad grow up to be adults in marriages trying to relearn that sex is actually really good. And not just in the giggly middle school way.

Some of our friends tell us that our kids are too young for these conversations. But I believe these conversations can change the world. They'll never be written up in newspapers or applauded on a big screen, but what if they prevent a single teen pregnancy or lead to less shame in marriage? What if talking openly about pornography saves my kids from seeking it out and absorbing its lies as some ultimate truth? What if learning about consent stops my sons from being in the paper one day for all the wrong reasons?

That last one is really important. My generation tried to prevent sexual assault by telling girls to dress modestly and not go out at night. When sexual violence was growing on college campuses, some universities responded by giving every female student a whistle. It was up to the victims to protect themselves. I'm not blaming anyone for these decisions. I know we're all just trying to do the best we can with the information we have. But I also know that our generation can and must do better.

So I started teaching my sons about consent very early on. Every parent knows this scenario: one moment your kids are having fun, and the next moment someone's crying. Their play fighting has devolved into real fighting. It's frustrating. And it's tempting to just tell them to stop fighting and move on. But this is also a powerful moment to pause and teach a deeper truth: "No means no" and "stop means stop."

I've said those words so often that my sons can parrot them back to me. They don't fully understand what I'm teaching them now, but I pray this lesson sticks: "Even if you seem to be having fun together at first, the moment someone says they don't like it anymore is the moment you stop."

We have to deal with our baggage about sex so we don't pass it on to our kids. When my daughter wears a top that shows her midriff, my instinct is to cover her up. But that's my baggage, not hers. It isn't fair to pass it on to her. I want her to be confident in her body, so I refuse to pass on any shameful messages about it.

If we don't want our children to feel shame about their bodies, then we need to model that for them. As Brené Brown says, "We need to be the adults we want our children to be."

Sex is normal. Sex is part of everyday life. But unpacking our own baggage about sex is hard. Having open conversations about sex is hard. It won't always be this way. If we push through the discomfort now, we'll be able to celebrate growth later. And, every once in a while, we'll get a glimpse of how our tough conversations are changing the world.

One night, my whole family was sitting around the dinner table, and this happened, completely unprompted:

My son Beckett (then five) with a sigh: "Dad, thanks for giving your sperm so that we could be here."

Me: "You bet, buddy." (Big thumbs up and obnoxiously large grin at my wife.)

Beckett, not done yet: "And mom, thanks for doing all the work. Cause Dad didn't do much. But you did the hard part. Thanks for getting us here alive."

Stacey: "You bet, buddy." (Subtle but undeniable smirk as my grin disappeared.)

Just another dinner table sex talk in our home. I know these talks won't always be so cute. As my kids grow, these talks may get awkward and uncomfortable, and brush up against my own shame. But if they allow my kids to feel confident in their bodies and teach them to celebrate sex as something good and holy and right, then these talks will be worth it.

# DUFFY

Duffy had been with our team for a long time. Everyone liked Duffy. By the time I first met him, he was a bit worn out and had surely seen better days. But he still performed his work passably well. That is, until we pushed him just a bit too far.

I hadn't seen Duffy for a while, but a few days before a big conference in Las Vegas, I knew it was time to find him. Duffy's specialty was carrying the fifty pounds of supplies we needed for our conference booth. So I pulled Duffy, our large, trusted duffle bag, from the storage closet and filled him with the various banners and signage I would need for the conference.

Dragging Duffy from the car to the airport check-in required balance and patience. Thankfully, he had sturdy wheels and I'd had lots of practice. When I was finally freed from my burden, I breezed through security and was soon on the plane. After landing in Vegas, I made my way to the baggage carousel. That's when everything fell apart. Literally.

Duffy didn't show. It took me a while to realize it. I kept staring at that conveyer belt, willing it to spit Duffy out. Finally, I could no longer ignore that I was the only one still standing there. I admitted defeat and made my way to the little baggage claim booth. The man asked for my flight information and baggage claim ticket. He tapped it into the computer and then his face fell. His mouth went a bit slack around the edges, and he looked at me with pain in his eyes. "I'll be right back," he muttered. Oh boy.

A few minutes later, I saw him returning with a luggage cart. There on the cold, hard steel was Duffy. I don't know what sort of monster tried to eat him, but he was looking rough, with multiple gaping holes. Poor, poor Duffy. We had finally pushed his tensile strength to the limit.

The airport attendant was very apologetic and explained how to lodge a complaint. I dutifully filled out the paperwork and then stared at Duffy, trying to make a plan. How was I going to haul fifty pounds of conference supplies through my massive casino hotel with a shredded bag? "Do you have anything to help me package this up?" I asked hopefully.

The man brought out some industrial-strength tape. For a moment, our eyes jumped between the bag, the supplies, the tape, and each other. Then we commenced the most awkward wrestling match ever seen as one of us tried to wrap our arms around Duffy and the other applied tape like caulk on a geyser. It wasn't pretty, but somehow we got the job done.

I was staying at one of those absurdly nice casinos. It was like a small city. For those on the Fitbit bandwagon, you could rack up thousands of steps just walking through it. So, when the taxi dropped me off, I was facing a long hike through a crowded casino with a ridiculously hobbled-together bag that no longer had functioning wheels. It was equal parts exhausting and embarrassing.

Somehow I made it to my hotel room. And somehow I made it to the conference the next day. Duffy had fallen apart, but he'd kept all of our supplies intact. The next few days were a swirl of people and talks and handshakes. Besides breaking Duffy, it ended up being a fairly successful trip.

It wasn't until I was packing everything up that I realized the error of my ways. There was no way I could get all of the supplies stuffed back into poor, broken-down Duffy. I'd barely crammed them all in on the way there. I eventually jammed it all in as well as I could and tried to come up with an alternative plan. In the end, I settled on having the hotel ship the bag home so I wouldn't have to mess with hauling it to the airport. But I still had to face the treacherous path from the packed-up conference booth to the (very far away) shipping office.

So, there I was in the middle of this beautiful hotel with amazing chandeliers overhead and hundreds of people gambling and sipping fancy drinks all around me. And I'm holding this monstrosity of a bag in a giant bear hug. I thought things couldn't get any worse. And then Duffy burst open like the world's worst pinata. Conference supplies spilled out on the patterned carpet, and people gasped and scrambled away from me like I had the plague.

With mounting desperation, I shoved things back in the hole, gripped it shut, and took a few more steps before a new hole formed. Then the entire cycle started all over again. It was absurd. I was like Hansel and Gretel leaving my trail of conference supplies behind me. Every time I picked something up, something else would fall out. It was a losing battle.

My anger grew with each step. I was angry that the bag that was nonfunctional at the start of the conference was still nonfunctional by the end of it. I could've ordered a new bag on Amazon, bought one in a store, or paid for someone to fix it. I hadn't done any of that. I was holding on to Duffy even though he no longer served a purpose. I had refused to fix him or let him go, and now I was suffering as a result. I wish I could say it was the only time I had allowed something like that to happen. But it wasn't.

Some of the most significant sources of pain in my life have come when I refused to slow down and acknowledge the work that needed to be done. I didn't want to face the reality of my situation, and then I got mad when my life split open at all the wrong times and all the wrong places. I usually wasted even more energy trying to shove stuff back in rather than actually dealing with the real problems I was carrying with me.

The writer of Ecclesiastes was right. There is a season for everything. What works now won't always work later. It's up to us to recognize when it's time to let go, move on, change tactics, and figure out how to move through life in a new way. Holding on can be a sign of strength and courage. But so can letting go when something no longer serves a helpful purpose.

# GARIBA

The sun beat down on me, the shade from the mango tree offering little relief from the stifling heat. I felt like a very sweaty version of MC Hammer in my baggy, brightly colored clothes. Hundreds of people I didn't know were speaking a language I didn't understand. There was yelling and chanting and sweating. So much sweating. This is one of my favorite memories in Makongo.

I had first arrived at this rural Ghanaian village several years before, when we were trying to find a home base for Mercy Project, the nonprofit I founded to rescue children from slavery. We picked Makongo because of its convenient location and friendly vibe. It was a very small village, and we were a very small organization, and I was a very small person coming from very far away. So, somehow, it all seemed to fit—even though they'd only had electricity for a few years before we showed up.

Over the years, Mercy Project and Makongo developed together. The organization built a home base and hired many of the local villagers to work on a big construction project. We added staff, and some of them found careers. Eventually, four of my close friends moved to Makongo to live in the home we built and to build the mission of Mercy Project, day by day. They were utterly dependent on the villagers. My friends stumbled on the language, the culture, and the customs. The villagers taught them with patience, kindness, and wisdom. In this way, the nonprofit and the village buoyed and strengthened each other as their progress intertwined, and they all pursued a shared vision of success.

Mercy Project entered Makongo with a sincere desire to live alongside people in a way that would lift us all up. We weren't there to show them how to live better. We were there to grow stronger together. I most certainly failed in those efforts at different points along the way. After all, I was twenty-seven years old when I started Mercy Project. I had no international experience and very little life experience to guide me. I jumped in to tackle the huge problem of child slavery with gusto and a bullheaded focus on results.

My courage and drive are some of my greatest strengths, but they also go hand in hand with my greatest weakness. My stubbornness, pride, and can't-waste-time attitude can lead to less-than-ideal outcomes. So, without meaning to, I'm sure I brought some layer of a white savior complex into Makongo. But my hope is that my intent to come alongside that community and recognize their inherent value outweighed any of the baggage I unwittingly carried with me.

Every time I visited Makongo, I met with the Chief. He was a serious but kind man with a great smile. In one of our meetings, he said that he would make me a sub-chief as a symbol of appreciation for what I, and Mercy Project, had done in their community. They would call me Gariba, which means Chief of Development. I didn't pronounce Gariba correctly, and I didn't feel worthy of this honor, but I knew that every chance for further connection should be taken. And so I gratefully accepted my new post.

I was struck by the lofty title, Chief of Development. I didn't know what development meant to the Chief or to the other villagers of Makongo, but for me, it meant making friends in a faraway place and attempting to offer them some of the opportunities I'd been offered in my own life. Development involves showing up over and over and over and sharing meals and sharing prayers, even in different languages and across different religions. But most of all, it means sharing a desire for everyone to have a chance. That's what united the villagers of Makongo with the team from Mercy Project—a shared desire for people to have a fair chance to work, grow, and develop. Together.

After I accepted my new title, I learned that the village of Makongo really knows how to throw a party. Everyone jumped in to help prepare for the big event. The women of the village sewed a special outfit for me to wear. Drummers from the next town over were hired to play. The Chief and other sub-chiefs prepared speeches and named the date and time. On the advice of some local friends, I even bought a cow to be presented as a gift of thanks during the ceremony (and killed at the end of the ceremony!).

When the big day arrived, Mercy Project staff and Makongo villagers gathered beneath the mango tree and sang and danced and clapped, an energy of hopefulness and gratitude filling the air. People sprinkled baby powder on us as the sweat came pouring down. Others stuck money on the drummers' damp foreheads as they worked hard to drive the music forward. Together, we declared a new day, one filled with possibilities that didn't exist before.

I felt so humbled and grateful to be part of that community and so amazed each time someone referred to me as Gariba. Standing up there, receiving that accolade, soaking in that applause was equal parts awesome and awkward. Besides the sweat and the baggy clothes, there was another reason I felt uncomfortable under that mango tree. I was grateful for the honor but also keenly aware of the hundreds of people who deserved to be up there with me. I was accepting the title of Gariba on behalf of everyone who had sacrificed, worked hard, and given of themselves to make Mercy Project a reality. Many of those are people whose names will never be known, and some of them I had never even thanked, either because I forgot or because I didn't even know what they had done.

When the light began to fade and it was time to leave, the village warrior insisted on escorting me down to Volta Lake. He wore leather work gloves and firmly gripped a rifle as he stoically escorted the newly instated Gariba to the riverbanks. There was no way that I could adequately thank him or the Chief or anyone else for the joy of that day. It was impossible to explain what it felt like to straddle two worlds, bolstered and encouraged by people on both sides.

I've had a number of titles in my life, but Gariba is one of the most meaningful. It taught me that everyone is at some stage of development. Everyone is hungry for the opportunity to be known as the very best version of themselves. Everyone needs someone to take the time to see their potential, call it forth, and grow alongside them.

# IMAGINARY FRIENDS

You've probably seen the meme that says, "Sometimes it seems like Jesus's greatest miracle is that he had twelve close friends in his thirties." That may have been written in jest, but it's not wrong. I'm sure many of you can relate. Jesus's inner circle loved him, knew him, and spent an abundance of time with him. In my loneliest seasons, that's a miracle I've longed for even if I didn't always have the language to name it.

We all crave connection—deep, real human connection. We were made for it. But somehow, when we get a few years out of college and start creeping closer to middle age, it no longer seems appropriate to plan our own playdates. So instead of making time for real-life get-togethers, our focus subtly shifts to curating our Instagram posts or growing our Facebook following or solidifying our LinkedIn presence. We trade real friends for virtual ones.

Social media is a safe way to make quasi-friends. Since they're not real friends, they can never really hurt us. Unfortunately, they can never really help us either. Our online friendships may have fewer downsides, but they also have virtually no upside.

I remember when my kids had imaginary friends. They were like training wheels for real relationships. Having an imaginary friend gave them something to hold on to when they wanted or needed a companion, even if it wasn't based in reality. Virtual friends are like imaginary friends for grown-ups. If we have thousands of followers and our posts get lots of likes, then we can say we're not lonely. We have people who understand us. We have people to hang out with. Except we don't.

In reality, we've traded real friends for fake ones. One costs nothing and the other costs our comfort. Why is it easier to have a thousand friends we don't really know than one who will actually show up for us? Because real friendship takes a lot of time and intentionality—and comes with the risk of being rejected or hurt or both.

If you're anything like me, the idea of deepening adult friendship feels overwhelming or exhausting or frankly impossible to add to an already overbooked schedule. And if that's the case, then I think we need to acknowledge that something is broken. I don't mean that we're broken; I'm talking about the way we consider deep, meaningful friendships to be optional. Humans need relationships like we need air: we can't spend any length of time on earth without either.

As long as those of us who crave depth and authenticity and realness fill our days to the brim with task after task after task, nothing about our loneliness is going to change. We've always had twenty-four hours in a day. That's not a new phenomenon. The new phenomenon is how we've packed those days so full of things that we have to schedule in the most mundane activities just so we can make sure we complete them. Eat lunch: done! Pick up kids from school: done! Go to the bathroom: done!

In a culture that values quantity over quality, it's not surprising that we would find ourselves with a dearth of deep relationships.

And in a world where nearly everything has been optimized for speed, it's hard to accept that there is no one-minute hack for instant friendship.

We all long for depth but have no idea where to find it. We're waiting for a magical moment: a long weekend at the beach, a guys' ski trip, or four girlfriends having babies in the same month. The reality is that's not how real friendships are forged.

Real friendships are more likely to be forged over PB&J sandwiches in the junior high football bleachers, or quick meetups at the grocery store before we rush back to our treadmill lives. There's no shortcut to depth. We need to purposely invest in the people we want in our lives. That's really hard to do when we spend hours every day watching Netflix or doom-scrolling through social media.

Our online friends often heighten our hunger for real friends. As we scroll through our feeds, it seems like everyone else is going on multiple vacations a year with the friends they've known since kindergarten! We look at them and wonder, *What's wrong with me? Why don't I have that?* The truth is that is not what's really happening in real life for almost anyone. Yet, sometimes in our gnawing desire for deeper friendships, we can overstate the magic of what other people seem to have.

If we don't have the kind of friendships we crave, then we need to ask ourselves why and at what cost. Beyond our busy schedules, fear of rejection may also be holding us back. Might we put ourselves out there in search of more meaningful adult friendships and get turned down? Certainly. But that's the whole point, isn't it? If there wasn't an option for the person to decline, would it really be an authentic relationship? I have no interest in co-opting someone to be my friend out of pity or obligation. That doesn't feel like real friendship to me.

There is risk in putting ourselves out there, but the greater risk is thinking that loneliness is the only option. It is simply not. It is the easier option, but that doesn't mean it's the only or most meaningful one.

I have a few adult friendships that have endured the test of time, and none of them happened by accident. We texted, called, and most importantly, carved time out of our busy schedules to be in person regularly, sometimes against all odds. We kept showing up through new babies, new jobs, new houses, and new seasons of life. In all of those instances, the friendships grew and became even more valuable as life got more complicated. The friendships made my life better, and sharing my life made those friendships richer.

One dear friend goes running with me nearly every weekend. Our friendship is based on a deep and sincere care for the other person that can only be born out of thousands of words shared over hundreds of hours. Occasionally we come into the weekly run with something specific to discuss, but more often we simply show up. As our feet fall into rhythm beneath us and the sun rises above us, our deepest struggles and questions and hopes rise from within us. No agenda, no set goals, no clear outcomes, no strategic planning—just two human beings who care enough about one another to keep showing up week after week.

Sometimes you don't realize how badly you need the shade from a tree until you finally have one to sit under. That's how I feel about my most meaningful and life-giving friendships. They sustain me, encourage me, and accompany me—a miracle that imaginary friends will simply never be able to provide.

# THE FIXER

Every few years, a small stone renders me useless. It turns out my kidneys are really good at making stones but not so good at passing them. So far, I've had three surgeries to remove them. That means I've had three separate experiences of lying in a hospital bed, hooked up to tubes, completely reliant on other people to care for me. I hate every second of it.

I can take the pain. I can take the disruption to my schedule. But I can't take how vulnerable it makes me feel.

In nearly every other situation in life, I find myself, or rather I position myself, as the fixer. I am almost always the thoughtful friend, the one who remembers big moments, the one who follows up, and the one other people call when something breaks (not literally, though, because I'm incredibly unhandy). I'm the one summoned to the hospital room at someone's worst moment. People call me when they are at wit's end with a complex personal or professional problem. I am frequently asked to give advice, lend support, and offer solutions. And I must say, it's far more enjoyable to be the one fixing than the one being fixed.

Being the fixer boosts my ego and validates my control issues. When my ability to fix, help, and control is used in service to others, it brings me a lot of praise. Playing the hero is fun for a while. But what do you do when a one-centimeter stone brings you to your knees? Or when your own damned needs, wants, and desires start to make themselves known? What happens when you realize that you need help, too?

I've gotten really good at hiding any evidence of needing help. I've declined help so many times that almost no one offers it anymore. I've trained everyone around me to believe that Chris Field doesn't need anything. And that's exactly what I wanted, right? Or so I thought.

The problem is that being a fixer is not just unhealthy but also unbelievably lonely. Fixers often feel like everyone needs our care but that no one cares about our needs (the ones we never admit to having, of course). And after long enough, we begin to wonder, *Would anyone actually show up for me the way I do for them?* At our very core, we know that people would, but we've never given them a chance. We've always pretended that we didn't need anyone else.

For those of us who have always been the fixers, the strong ones, the dependable ones, there's a real need for us to acknowledge that we've got some messed up stuff, too. It requires vulnerability and risk to name the needs that we've never even acknowledged to ourselves, much less other people.

When we find language to voice our needs for the first time, it can initially cause new challenges. We're forcing people to change patterns that have developed over decades. When the perceived fixer suddenly realizes they too need to be fixed, everyone has to learn a new role.

If someone in your life always takes on the role of doing the right thing and showing up for everyone else, it's possible that person has some real insecurity and fear around ever letting their guard down enough to actually be loved just for being. They've fixated on giving and found their worth there. And they are praised for it constantly, which complicates things even more.

Despite what they actually say (and even mostly mean) about being "fine," they're not really fine. "Fine" isn't the goal, anyway. To be "fine" or "okay" is the lowest possible bar there could be. If you really want to love the fixers well, you need to ask them a different question. "Are you okay?" or "Do you need anything?" won't get you any helpful information. Maybe the question should be "Do you feel safe enough to let me really see you?" But be prepared for silence the first time you ask. They've almost certainly never been asked this question before—which is exactly why it matters.

They probably are fine and okay, but it's not as certain that they feel safe. Don't take it personally; it's just never something that they've felt permission to feel. It's never the role they assumed or the part they were cast into. But if you give a person like that some space and you're persistent over time, you will discover that they do have some legitimate needs and that they desperately want to be seen as they are and loved just because.

Accepting love requires vulnerability. Accepting love for *who you are* and not *what you do* requires losing control. You're no longer the fixer. You are just loved for no reason other than being who you are. That feels so unreasonable to me. It leaves me thinking there must be something I can do to balance the scales. I want to justify the love I receive, to make it worth the giver's time, and to give them a good return on their investment. That's how business works, but that mindset is a poison for relationships. A poison many of us chug ourselves without being prompted.

I got another kidney stone as I was writing this book. I am, in this very moment, waiting on a call back from the urologist about getting a scan to see how large the stone is and whether it'll pass on its own or will require a fourth surgery.

I told several people about this stone. They all offered sincere prayers and concern, but one person outside of my family checked on me every day. Every single day for over a week. She carved out thirty seconds of time in her busy schedule to acknowledge my pain and offer her love, day after day after day. I had always known she loved me, but this time I felt it deeply. Perhaps it was the first time I had been vulnerable enough to receive her full love. For just a moment, I was able to sit and receive the genuine love of another human being with nothing expected in return. I think I need more of that in my life.

# THE NEXT LEVEL

When you run for mayor of your hometown at nineteen years old, people talk. When you start an international nonprofit that helps rescue over 250 children from human trafficking, people talk louder. When you write two bestselling books and become a TEDx speaker (twice over), people have all sorts of things to say:

> "Chris is so intense. I don't know how he does all of that."
>
> "Chris has such a crazy capacity. Look at what he's accomplished."
>
> "Chris operates at a different level."

Do you want to know how I kept reaching new levels? By worshiping at the altar of efficiency and making productivity my highest priority. I took my natural gifts of high energy, discipline, and ambition and pushed them to their absolute limit. I did a lot of cool things—but it came at a cost.

The dark side of my efficiency is that I was rarely present in my own life. I didn't know that at the time, of course, but I can see it so clearly now. I was always calculating and strategizing about how to get ahead, do more, and accomplish the newest challenge. Everything was about reaching the next level. Each task was merely a springboard to the next one. Each conversation was either a stepping stone or a stumbling block to the next important item on my list. I didn't mean to hurt anybody along the way, but I know I did.

My pace wasn't good for the people in my life. With productivity as my main metric of success, I was forever blowing past the people and places around me. There was no time for depth. There was little space for nuance. There was no value given to simply being with someone, listening deeply, or sharing vulnerably. My relationships were a mile wide and an inch deep. All in the name of efficiency.

My pace wasn't good for me either. Efficiency is exhausting. The treadmill never stopped, not when I took a lunch break, not when I went on vacation, not when I spent "quality" time with my family. Not even when I tried to go to sleep. There was always more to do. The faster I got, the farther I wanted to run. The more space I cleared on my schedule, the more tasks I rushed to fill it with.

It was like I was back in elementary school playing *Super Mario Bros*. You remember the original *Mario Bros.* on the original Nintendo, right? My parents challenged my sister and me to come up with half the money for one, promising they would cover the rest. We saved for months for that incredible machine. But instead of enjoying games like *Mario Bros.* and experiencing all of the amazing graphics, I was always on the lookout for shortcuts and secret warp zones.

My goal was to beat the game as quickly as possible with minimum effort. So I learned about every hack and skipped every possible level. That's how I learned how to go from level 1-2 to 4-1 and then from level 4-2 to 8-1. These hacks allowed you to beat the entire game while only actually playing about 25 percent of the levels. There were entire levels that I just completely missed because I was in such a rush to win. And what would I do then? Go buy a new game, of course. Ever in search of the next dopamine hit, I was too young to comprehend the true costs.

As a child, I had to keep beating video games so I could brag about it to my friends. The same thing was happening as an adult. All around me, I saw people who had gamified life. Everything was about getting to the next level. Somehow, we all believed the lie that if we could just get the better job, earn the higher salary, or move into the better neighborhood, then we would be satisfied, and it would be worth whatever pain it had cost us.

But then we got there and felt just as empty as we did before. So we had to set up a new challenge. On and on we all raced, endless loops on a vague path to somewhere important. Passing one another with a rushed "Doing good—just so busy!" as if it were a badge of honor or something happening to us, beyond our control.

When we obsess over efficiency and are forever desperate to reach the next level, our focus is on the big moments. We stack them up and squeeze them as tightly together as possible: the dream vacation, the lucrative promotion, the weddings, graduations, and anniversaries. We give no value to the slower, boring, sacred spaces in between.

We can be front row for our children's infrequent milestone memories but miss the mundane miracle of watching them become fuller versions of themselves day by day. We can have an amazing wedding, throw lavish anniversary parties, and plan romantic date nights, but our partners may still feel emotionally distant.

There is no efficient way to be a good partner or good parent. When we streamline story time, our kids feel our rush. When we ask "How was your day?" but don't listen to the answer, our spouses notice. And if you're like me, when you accomplish amazing things and still feel lost inside, you may start to realize:

> *There's always going to be a next level.*
>
> *Life is rushing by too quickly, and I'm missing what's truly important.*
>
> *I can't keep running.*
>
> *There has to be something more to life than efficiency and productivity.*
>
> *This treadmill will never stop or slow down until I have the courage to step off.*

We aren't made to go through life as quickly as possible. That was never the goal. It's literally not a race. We need other people alongside us. We need to feel seen, known, desired, and understood—and to give those gifts to others. And there is nothing efficient about that process. It is messy and time-consuming. There are no three-step plans or life hacks to get you there, but it's the level I'm finally ready to slow down long enough to reach.

# WHO DO YOU WANT TO BE?

I recently transitioned out of the day-to-day responsibilities in the organization that I founded in my late twenties. Now I'm forty years old and asking myself, "Who do I want to be when I grow up?" This question is equal parts terrifying and freeing.

As we grow up, the question "Who do you want to be?" becomes increasingly rare. At some point, it turns into "What do you want to do?" and then into "What are you doing today?" We get so focused on our overflowing schedules that we rarely take the time to consider who we actually want to be or who we are actually becoming.

If we did, I'm sure few of us would answer that we want to be the kind of adult who spends all of their time watching Netflix or who screams at their kid from the sideline of a baseball game or who is always working and never has time for their family. That can't just be me, right?

The problem isn't our answers; the problem is that we never ask in the first place. Instead of asking questions, we spend our lives on autopilot: we go through all the training and do the hard work to get the plane off the ground, but never stop to ask if we're headed to the right airport. We just keep forging ahead, letting the momentum of our lives carry us forward.

At least that's how I felt for the first forty years of my life. I was on a path to be a strong leader, loving husband, devoted father, world changer. Those were good goals, and I was making good progress toward them. But no one had told me that the goals could change along the way. No one had told me that I could wake up every single day and choose who I wanted to be and how I wanted to feel. No one had ever told me that no matter what happened today, I could make a different choice tomorrow.

And then someone did.

I was in the middle of a counseling session, listing out every possible job I could pursue. My mind was racing through the possibilities, trying to be as creative and exhaustive as possible as I considered all of my experiences and abilities. Then my therapist said, "I am more interested in how your work makes you feel, rather than what your job title might be."

This was a revelation: not only could I choose who I want to be; I could also choose how I want to feel. How I feel actually matters.

My feelings had never been a factor in my decision-making. I had spent such a long time completely divorced from my feelings, refusing to listen to them, never asking their advice. So I had no idea how work made me feel. I'd never thought about it before.

Trying to access that place inside of me requires a lot of self-reflection and intentionality. I'm now taking time to consider how different types of work will make me feel—a consideration I had never once prioritized. At age fourteen, I worked my very first job as a Little League umpire. When I was out there calling games under the brutal Texas sun, my main focus was earning enough money to buy some candy and maybe a new video game. Work was functional, a means to an end.

As I worked my way up from umpire to radio station assistant to pastor to nonprofit CEO to chief growth officer at a startup, work became functional in other ways. Whether I like to admit it or not, at some point prestige and clout and credibility became even more important than the number on my paycheck. Never once did I stop to question how any of that made me feel.

So, here I am, a middle-aged man, wondering who I want to be when I grow up. There are a number of things that I am capable of doing, but that's not how I'm setting the bar for this next season of my life. Just because I *can* do something doesn't mean I want to, need to, or should. Instead, I long to do work that feels meaningful, whether or not it draws the most applause, accolades, or, yes, even income.

Discovering the answers to this question is important, sacred work. It will set the tone for how I live the rest of my life. And these decisions aren't just for me but for my family and the example I set for my kids. Maybe one day, when my children are old enough that people ask them what their dad does, they won't answer with a job title or occupation but by describing how I choose to take up space in the world with intention, purpose, and clarity. Maybe they'll talk more about who I am than about who signs my paychecks.

# MY GREATEST FAILURE

You never know what will come up when you ask a group of college students, "Do you have any questions?" Even so, I try to end most of my lectures this way. One year, I was rewarded with a question that made me awkward and uncomfortable, launched me into weeks of deep soul-searching, and, ultimately, transformed me into a better human being. Let me explain.

I was teaching a class about using business to solve social problems, and I loved talking about how Mercy Project was improving the fishing industry in Ghana so that they didn't have to rely on child labor. After sharing that story one year, a student said: "It sounds like you've had a good amount of success on many of your ventures. Would you mind telling us about your greatest failure?" I wasn't expecting that. I stammered my way through a mediocre answer, feeling equal parts awkward and uncomfortable.

That experience plagued me for weeks. It was a simple question. Why didn't I have a better response? Why was it so painful to talk about my failures? Everyone makes mistakes. Why was I scared to talk about mine? We all know that no one is perfect and that everyone struggles. But because we rarely hear about other people's failures, we keep our own problems hidden, too.

As I was wrestling with my failure to talk about my failures, a line from one of my old college professors returned to me. At the time, I was applying for jobs as a church minister. This professor told us: "Churches don't mean to lie to you, but they do." He went on to explain that churches will tell you who they *want to be* and not who they *actually are*.

The same is true for all of us, isn't it? We don't mean to lie to each other, but we do. The narratives we share are so polished because we often tell people who we *want to be* and not who we *actually are*. We sanitize our stories and clean up our conversations. Most of us mislead in this way to one degree or another, and we're not exactly sure how to stop—mostly because we don't even realize how often we do it.

Telling the truth about our imperfections is terrifying. It takes immense social risk to actually own our shortcomings when no one else is doing it. When other people are bragging about how big of a fish they caught, it's hard to admit your own line got so tangled up that you never even cast it.

Despite my fear, I desperately want to be a truth teller. I think deep down, we all do. We admire people who are comfortable enough in their own skin to talk about the things that most of us keep locked away. There's something captivating and refreshing about being around people who tell the truth. It's a redemptive experience.

And the miraculous outcome is that truth begets truth. When we actually admit our weaknesses and warts and the really awful stuff about us, it emboldens other people to do the same. It allows us to connect with people at a level that is so much more authentic and genuine than most of us have ever experienced. You might even say it allows us to be fully human with one another in a way that just can't happen otherwise.

Perhaps this is why childhood friends are so dear to us. They saw us at our worst, most exposed moments and then kept showing up for us. There is a depth of truly knowing each other that carries us through the years. That's why we can go a long time without seeing our childhood friends and then catch back up right where we left off.

This is so different from the friendships we form as adults. As we get older, we tend to hide the parts of ourselves that we don't want others to see. We weren't sophisticated enough to do that when we were kids. Children say what they're thinking, and their friends either stick around or they don't. Children don't spend time wondering how they'll fit in or weighing their actions based on other people's reactions.

Adults often miss or even actively avoid opportunities to speak openly with others about the hard parts of life. It's not that we purposefully tell disingenuous narratives, but we do shy away from total honesty. It makes us feel too vulnerable. So we rely on half-truths, white lies, and vague responses. I wonder how different our relationships would be if we actually named and acknowledged our truths.

The sad thing is that we often don't even tell the truth about all the good things we feel. We hesitate to admit when joy, delight, and gratitude well up in us. Recently, I was chatting with an acquaintance after my daughter was in a musical at her school. I don't know this man very well. We were just making small talk as dozens of other people milled around us. Then he looked right at me and said, "You know, this is the good stuff in life. Moments like this make life great." His statement shocked me. Of course, he was absolutely right. We had just seen a group of kids pour their hearts out, sharing their gifts and enjoying the fruit of all of their hard work. It really was an amazing experience, but I doubt anyone else in that crowded room said something like that, especially to someone they barely knew. But he felt something, and he said it. Social risk be darned.

We often stay shallow and then lament that our relationships have no depth. How can we expect deep relationships if we've never had honest conversations? The only way to have deep human connections is to be honest about the best and the worst parts of ourselves and our lives. This is risky, but the reward makes it worthwhile. When we show up as our authentic selves, we give others permission to be real, too. We become like magnets, drawing others into deeper connections.

If I wanted to be a truth teller, then I couldn't only tell my class about my wins and ignore all of my losses. I had to talk about my failures, too. It took me a few weeks to build up the courage, but eventually, I brought up the topic again. I spent ten minutes talking about some of my biggest failures, both personally and as a leader. It was good for my soul, and I'd like to think it was good for theirs too.

# TELLING THE TRUTH

Kids are pretty obvious when they lie. They stomp their feet and promise they didn't eat the cake, even though chocolate is smeared all over their mouths. They angelically assure you they would never hit their brother, even though you just saw it happen. Their lies are direct and often a bit ridiculous.

We adults are a bit of a different story, aren't we? We rarely *mean* to lie. We rarely *plan* to lie. And we definitely don't want to be known as liars. But many adults have a tricky relationship with the truth. At least I know I do.

When I turned forty, I spent some time really evaluating who I was and how I was living my life. One thing I discovered is how often I skirted the truth. My reasons were always pretty noble (or at least pretty noble-sounding). I'd tell little white lies to avoid disagreements or hurt feelings or discomfort. And I had developed all the mental gymnastics needed to tap dance around the truth.

But that's not who I want to be anymore. I want to be a truth teller. I want my internal dialogue to match my external discussions. I want to be authentic, even if it sometimes means being uncomfortable.

The biggest truths I held back were my own. I struggled to name my needs. I lacked the courage to say when I was hurt, disappointed, or confused. And I hated speaking up when my expectations weren't met. It was always easier to say I was "fine" than to speak my full truth. It was easier, but it wasn't better—because I certainly wasn't fine. And those lies always cost something. Even pennies add up when you collect enough of them over many years.

I also held back from sharing what I truly thought about others. My old filter used to be *How will other people feel if I say that?* as if it was my job to protect their feelings. There were times when I knew something was happening in a friend's life, but I didn't have the guts to speak plainly about it. I could tell things were tense with their spouse, but who was I to bring it up? I could see they were going down a destructive path, but I didn't want to have a hard conversation.

It took a while for me to find a better filter. I didn't want to go so far in the other direction that I started to use the truth as a sledgehammer. Then I read a quote by Brené Brown, "Clear is kind. Unclear is unkind." Yes! That's how I wanted to move through the world: with clarity and kindness. I used to think kindness meant avoiding painful conversations. I was wrong. Clear is kind. So many people are hungry for clarity. I know I am.

Asking myself *Is this clear? Is this kind?* before I speak has led to some difficult conversations. But I've been surprised by how often people are genuinely grateful that I took the time to be clear with them. Sometimes they'll even respond, "Yes, I know that's true. I just needed someone to say it to me." They appreciate the external validation of someone else acknowledging the problem.

That's not to say that these kinds of conversations always go well. One time in my early twenties, I was the recipient of someone being clear, and I completely blew up and went on the defensive. What they said was absolutely true. I just didn't want to hear it. So rather than face the truth, I lashed out and belittled them.

That conversation was a double whammy. Not only was I rude and immature, but I also missed the opportunity to grow and better myself. My inability to handle their comments didn't just result in an embarrassing response but also led to future unnecessary pain. So I know firsthand that speaking the truth doesn't always feel good in the moment, but I also know that the risk is worth it.

My journey toward truth has involved a lot of lament. I've mourned the times I haven't accepted the truth from others. And I've mourned the times I haven't been clear with those around me. This only strengthens my conviction to continue being clear and kind and truthful. I want to make clarity and kindness a cornerstone of all of my relationships. Even when it's uncomfortable. *Especially* when it's uncomfortable—because I'm convinced the world needs more kind truth tellers.

# A NEW BLUEPRINT

I remember the butterflies in my stomach when I first told my girlfriend (now wife) that I loved her. We were eighteen and sixteen, and I knew deep in my soul that I loved her. I didn't yet fully comprehend exactly what that meant or how many years-turned-decades we would work to grow that little spark of love into something bigger, but I knew I loved her. So I took a deep breath and said, "I love you." And thank God she smiled that day and said it right back. But it doesn't always go that way.

"I love you" is a risk. What if they don't feel the same way? What if they don't want your love? Saying those three little words can make you feel vulnerable and scared and hopeful all at once. But when you put your heart out there, and the other person accepts it and gives you their love in return, well, that's the best feeling in the world.

"I feel loved by you" is also a risk—one that few people take. Instead, we say, "Thank you," or "That's so nice," or "Appreciate it," even when those words don't come close to expressing the depth of what we actually feel.

Maybe the problem is that there's no blueprint for these kinds of conversations. The leading man says, "I love you," and the movie score swells in the background. But we can't imagine that same man telling a new friend, "What you did made me feel so loved. I'm grateful that you're in my life."

Since embracing the mantra "Clear is kind," I've tried to practice telling someone right there in the moment when they've made me feel safe or seen or loved. If I sense a deeper connection, I want to name it, even (and especially) if it's someone I haven't known for a long time. Since there's no blueprint for this level of connection, I thought I'd share the one I've been working on.

When I call customer service and the representative is exceptionally helpful, I make sure to say, "I hope your manager is listening to this call because it is really clear to me that you take pride in doing a good job, and you've done that today. Thank you for your kindness and professionalism." Those are the easier ones because I don't see their faces, and I'll never interact with them again. It gets harder when it's someone closer to me. The stakes are higher.

When I spend time with someone and feel a meaningful connection, I'll tell them, "There's something about being with you that makes me feel really valued. I sense a shared energy here, and I'm really grateful for it." Sometimes that sort of declaration leads to an awkward pause. Sometimes the other person gets flustered and doesn't know how to respond. But most of the time, they smile and say, "Me too," and we share a depth of connection that feels rare and special and life-giving.

Of course, I try to carry this clear, kind language into my family as well. It's easier there because I've always freely told them, "I love you." But now I try to really express the details of my love. So, when I'm praying with my kids before bed, I thank God for the honor of watching them grow up, and I express how grateful I am to spend part of every day with them. And rather than rushing out the door in the mornings with a quick "Love you," I'm learning to pause and tell my wife how much I truly appreciate her and what a gift she is to me and everyone around her.

As I follow this blueprint, I realize that the feelings have been there all along. I don't have to conjure them up or force them into existence. They're inside me, clear as can be. I just have to put in the effort to share them with others. It's like those connect-the-dots activity pages. The dots are there, but you have to take the time to draw the line. That's when the picture appears. That's when the magic happens.

This kind of vulnerability pushes some people away and draws others closer. But the thing is, we don't get to choose which will happen in any given moment from any given conversation. And we can certainly play it safe, but we'll be playing it alone. That doesn't feel worth it to me. So I'll keep taking a deep breath and saying how I really feel and let the cards fall where they may.

# THE MIDDLE WAY

We are in a culture war. Pick a side: Good or evil? Right or terribly wrong? Your choice will determine everything. At least that's what we hear on the news every day.

It's like we're all playing a giant game of Red Rover. But instead of people clasping their hands to keep you out, they're desperately trying to pull you in. Neither side wants you to remain in the middle because the side with the most people wins. So we're acting like we did in elementary school; the only difference is that the name-calling has gotten a lot worse.

People who try to stay in the middle are yelled at a lot. They're hated by the left and by the right. They're demeaned for their unwillingness to choose. If the risk of choosing one side is losing the other, then the risk of choosing neither side is losing them all. The middle can be a lonely place, even a dangerous one. I know because that's where I most often stand.

I've spoken out for years about the third, fourth, fifth, tenth, and umpteenth way of looking at issues like racism, gender, abortion, the death penalty, gun control, and more. It's brought me ire from both sides. I've lost real friends over it. I'm often not progressive enough for my progressive friends and not conservative enough for my conservative friends. They say I lack conviction, but I'm actually acting out of a deep conviction. They're just mad that it doesn't overlap with theirs.

The truth is that there are always more than two options. You can care about racial injustice without being anti-police. And supporting the police doesn't make you racist. And on and on I could go (and probably make some of you throw this book across the room in a fit of rage). But I won't shout at you about the middle way. I won't try to force you to see it as intensely as people from either side try to force you *not* to see it.

If you're like me, you're tired of being shouted at. The endless tug-of-war and childish games of Red Rover are exhausting. Even reading these first few paragraphs may have made your body tense and your mind race.

The middle is not a place of shouting or forcing or point-making. It is a place of deep listening. We don't listen defensively or in hopes of catching the other person's mistake. In the middle, we listen with empathy and sincere interest and curiosity. We listen with a desire to understand. A *true* desire to understand.

When we listen like that, we will find that people on very different sides of hot-button issues can make compelling points. And if we don't agree, or even adamantly disagree, we can at least try to understand where they're coming from. We can trace their journey back, hoping to see how they arrived at their conclusions. This is an exercise in both empathy and compassion.

The closer I listen, the more I realize that the people yelling the loudest are often the most wounded. They shout about their views so they don't have to explore the hatred and pain and fear within them. If I want them to honor my conviction about the middle way, then I must be willing to listen to them, too. Even when I don't really want to. Maybe especially then.

I was introduced to the middle way when I opened myself to learning, listening, and engaging with people who are vastly different from me. They showed me new ways of moving through the world. I realized that it's foolish to only listen to the narratives that echo my own and only see people whose lives parallel mine. When we only see, hear, and speak about one side of an issue, then it's far too easy to ignore logic and confuse opinions with facts.

It is a sign of maturity and wisdom not to try and force every person we meet to see the world exactly like we do. It is a further sign of maturity and wisdom when we actually find it dangerous to surround ourselves only with people who view and experience the world exactly like we do. If these kinds of echo chambers make you nauseous, then you might be ready for the middle way.

Finding the middle way isn't easy. At first, the path will feel like it needs to be created with machetes, and we'll fear stepping on a snake at any moment. *There is a clear and wide road close by*, we'll think. *Why don't I just take it?* And certainly that would be the smoother path.

But then we'll remember the kind of world we want for our children and grandchildren: a colorful world that has moved beyond black-and-white thinking. We'll remember that every important road was first cleared with machetes, and the snakes will flee when we uncover their hiding places. So we'll find our courage and keep going.

Those of us on the middle way shouldn't keep this conviction to ourselves. Even though it feels risky, we must keep talking about this path we're on, offering it up as a map for others to follow. We can show that it's possible not to choose a side at the expense of patronizing and belittling the other. We can share the power of saying, "I don't want to play this game anymore." We can use our voices and influence and platforms to speak with conviction about the middle way.

The middle way can be a lonely, grueling path. But the longer I stay on it, the less lonely it becomes. I keep talking about it, and more and more people are willing to listen. More and more people are uncomfortable with the options that exist and desperate to find another way. More and more people don't want to look at the world from a singular point of view.

If you want to find the middle way, you will. It may be different than what you hoped, wanted, or believed your path would be. But if you seek the middle way with intention and an open mind and a willingness to embrace the world, then you'll find it. And you'll discover the freedom and joy of living away from each side's shadow.

Until more of us find this path and blaze this trail, people will continue to believe that they only have two options. They'll hold their breath and choose one, stuffing down their concerns and blindly accepting the current rules of the game. I refuse to do that anymore. How about you?

# ALARM BELLS

I've been to Houston's huge international airport too many times to count. Walking through the terminals always brings a cacophony of sights, sounds, and smells. But the last time I was there, something new and unexpected took me by surprise and gave me a lot to think about.

Up until that point in my trip, everything had gone according to plan. I had arrived at the airport early and made it through security in record time. My shoes were already back on my feet, and my laptop was snug in my bag. I was heading toward my gate when it happened.

Suddenly, bright white lights flashed on every wall, and a shrill alarm filled the air. I instinctively froze, trying to understand what was going on. Then a robotic voice came through the loudspeakers: "A fire alarm has been activated. Please exit safely." Feeling both tense and terrified, I prepared to run for my life.

Then I looked around me. No one else was reacting at all. Hundreds of people kept speed walking through the concourse. They continued with their regularly scheduled plans, completely uninterested in the warning signs surrounding us. Instead of responding to the alarm bells, they just kept streaming through security, walking toward their gates, and buying overpriced food.

I now had a choice to make. Would I be the one weirdo running toward the exits, or would I join in the mass delusion? I chose the latter. My reasoning went like this: I'm not going to be concerned if no one else is concerned. For a moment, I paused to wonder if people were looking at me thinking the same thing. But I brushed that thought aside and continued on to my gate.

Each step solidified my resolve to simply ignore all the alarm bells. I had important places to go, important people to see, and a tight schedule to check off all of my important tasks. A forced evacuation did not fit into my plans. That line of thinking made it easier to pretend that everything was fine.

Eventually, I boarded the plane and flew away without ever seeing smoke, fire, or flames. I'm still not sure what happened at that airport, but the whole experience left me rattled. There was something oddly familiar about the situation. As it turns out, I've had plenty of practice ignoring alarm bells in my life. I think many of us have.

There's this tendency to just keep pushing ourselves through life. When something feels off, we just ignore it. Maybe it's a relationship in need of repair or a church that no longer seems to fit or a job that daily leaves us frustrated and angry. We wake up in the middle of the night with a gut feeling that something isn't right, but we push those thoughts away and numb ourselves back to sleep. Then we wake up in the morning, force our feet onto the floor, and keep tumbling forward without ever stopping to address the parts of our lives that just clearly aren't working anymore.

So many of us have alarm bells going off about unhealthy tendencies in our lives: our screen addiction, our mounting debt, our impatient parenting, and even signs of distress in our own body. We know that we're not good stewards of the very container we've been given to get us through the rest of our lives. The way we feel at the end of the day and the way we feel after meals and the way we feel when we climb too many stairs—we know it's not good or healthy or desirable. But since no one else is talking about it, we decide not to respond either.

What would it have taken for me to listen to those alarm bells? Did I need to see smoke, flames, firefighters? Would I still be standing there, staring at everyone else while the airport burned down around me?

The problem with modeling our lives after the examples of others is that there are a lot of unhealthy, miserable people in the world. We all tell each other that we're fine. That herd mentality keeps us stumbling forward regardless of the results. Who is going to have the courage to say, "I'm not fine"? Who is willing to say, "This isn't what I want. This isn't how I want to feel"? Who is going to admit they're tired of following in other people's unhealthy footsteps?

One of my favorite quotes is "Easy choices, hard life. Hard choices, easy life." I cannot shake that truth. It has stuck in my brain for so long. The easy choice when we hear an alarm is to take our cues from everyone else and simply do nothing. Eventually, that will make our lives really hard. Or we can make the hard choice to respond to those alarms. We can swim upstream like those salmon in Alaska because we know in our guts that it will lead us to an easier, healthier, more authentic life.

My airport experience made me realize just how often I'm ignoring the alarm bells in my own life. The times my stress from work carries over into how I speak to my children. The times my foolish pride keeps me from being a good husband. The times I refuse to make the small, daily decisions to steward my body and mind well. Each of these moments sets off an alarm bell telling me that the road I'm walking on is not ultimately where I want to go.

Those alarm bells offer a choice. I can either stop, listen, and change direction, or I can keep on walking, whistling louder to drown out that little alarm in my head telling me this isn't who I want to be. It's one thing to never hear an alarm. But it's on me when I hear and see them and still choose to do nothing.

# THE DARKEST NIGHT

*Mark this page for your worst day. If you are in a deep, dark space, then you may feel less alone on these pages. If you're humming along and things are going great, save this for the next time the wind gets knocked out of you.*

Disaster struck my world this week. Sorrow and pain flooded in, and I'm wading through the wreckage. If I were someone who used alcohol to numb myself, I would've made my way to many liquor stores in the last week. If I used drugs to numb myself, there would have been nights I didn't come home at all. If I used food to numb myself, they would've had to bring truckloads of Blue Bell ice cream to my door.

Instead, I numb myself by being busy, filling my days with mindless tasks that allow me to pretend I'm in control. If I get moving fast enough, I can emotionally disconnect from what's happening around me. Life becomes a blur, and there's no time for the horrific thoughts to take hold. But eventually, I have to stop. All the tasks are finished. All the distractions are gone. And now I am all alone.

My world has shattered, but who can I tell? Who can I trust to bear this bad news with me? Who is safe enough to allow into my inner circle? The deeper the cut, the shorter the list gets.

Sometimes solitude is a wonderful escape, but sometimes solitude is like being choked. At first, this silence was like a pair of handcuffs, and now it has become a cell where I am trapped, all alone. I know people are just a phone call away, but I'm scared to reach out for help. The pity in their eyes, the pointless platitudes, the pained glances—being alone seems like the safer option. It's not true, but deep in my soul, it feels as true as the sun coming up every morning.

It seems extraordinarily risky to share this tragedy with another human being. I can barely handle it myself. I don't want to burden anyone else. It would be unkind to drag someone into this mess, like inviting them into a rainstorm when they've been enjoying blue skies. At least these are the stories I tell myself.

The irony is that when I've been welcomed into someone else's darkest moments, I'm honored that they've trusted me to hold their pain. Sometimes it's a pain I can't hold, and they just ask me to hold them while they bear the pain. I've never once felt annoyed, upset, or burdened when someone invited me into their darkness. But it sure is easier to be invited in than to be the one handing out invitations.

Some people live in this darkness all the time. Maybe it's their mental health, or maybe it's their difficult life circumstances, but this week I've gained a whole new level of empathy for them. It reminds me that it's really hard to see someone in a ditch and understand why they feel so hopeless, dejected, and broken down there. It may appear very straightforward to someone on the outside: "Why not just come out of that ditch?" Nah, that's not it. Now I realize. Now I remember. My pain throbs, and my empathy grows—a consolation prize I can't yet appreciate.

Pain is a reminder that life is fragile and unfair. We have a lot less control over both the best and worst days than we like to admit. When everything you hold on to for strength, confidence, and comfort gets ripped away, you realize that control is just a grown-up pacifier.

You can structure and plan your life until it is as finely tuned as a first-class orchestra, but none of that matters when disaster strikes. It's like you're the conductor onstage, commanding everyone, "We are going to play this song, and every string and every note will be exactly what it needs to be. There shall be no dissent, no challenges, no objections. Nothing can go wrong here."

Then you bow to the audience and turn around to face your perfectly positioned orchestra, and a hole opens up in the floor and you're falling into the void at a thousand miles an hour without a parachute. At that point, it doesn't matter how closely you tuned your violin or how your tuxedo looks or how many times you practiced the crescendo: now all that matters is surviving.

We have fallen for a mirage. Our lives cannot be controlled. I've denied that truth, willing myself to believe that if I just keep showing up, things will keep working out. We hear it in sermons. We hear it in Bible studies. People say it in good faith every day. They hope that if they say it enough, it will be true. But it's not.

Tragedy is part of the full human experience. It's harder than we want to admit. It can make us feel alone and defeated. But it is important to dig in and actually feel it. Strategies for numbing the pain won't move us toward healing. The only cure is to name the woundedness and invite others into it. By unlocking our doors, we can help others unlock theirs too. That doesn't make me feel any better, but it's the truth.

In this life we can't avoid pain. The best we can do on our deep, dark nights is not walk through them alone. Maybe that's really the only thing we can control. On our darkest nights, we don't have to wait for the sun by ourselves.

# UNBECOMING

Far too many of us live inauthentic lives. There are artists in business school because their parents told them to chase the American dream. There are writers who went into medicine because "that's what smart people do." There are people who hate their jobs because they took the first one they found and have been too scared to leave.

So many of us don't know who we are or what we want or who we were intended to be. We never asked ourselves those questions because the answers never mattered. Our true selves weren't valued. But we can only live off the fuel of other people's plans for so long before we inevitably crash. And so many of us are crashing. The wreckage is all around us.

My crash is still happening. Little screws popping off, nails coming undone, wood bending and breaking. It's a gradual unbecoming. If the first half of my life was about building an impressive facade, the second half is about dismantling it piece by piece. This is terrifying, exhilarating work. And it's impossible to do if I continue to use the opinions of others as a barometer of my success.

Somewhere along the way, I picked up the idea that having my own thoughts and feelings and preferences is somehow selfish. I think it's pretty common for those of us raised in certain Christian subcultures. You are "good" if you follow the rules, accept the conventions, and toe the party line. You are "bad" if you question authority, disrupt the status quo, and form your own opinions. So you're constantly scanning your environment, measuring yourself against others, and making sure you fit in.

For forty years, I have cared deeply what people think about me. I have made many important decisions based solely on how I will be perceived. I have regularly turned away from what I truly wanted to avoid the pain of sticking out or drawing criticism. But I don't want to do that anymore.

Part of my unbecoming is learning to engage the world on my own terms—no apology or explanation needed. I'm unlearning the lie that being authentic is the same as being selfish. I know that's not true. You can be a unique person and still care about others. You can be true to yourself and still have healthy relationships with people starkly different from you. That's a sign of maturity.

I'll take it one step further. I believe true maturity means being comfortable knowing that most people around us, including the people we love the most, will almost certainly view both the mundane and often the hot-button issues very differently than we do. And instead of treating that as a threat, we can embrace it as something that adds beauty to the world.

If somebody votes differently, prays differently, spends money differently, sends their kids to school differently, or engages their community differently, *that's okay*. We can still love them. We can still befriend them. We can still approach them with curiosity and kindness. When we're comfortable and confident in our own skin, we don't have to live in fear that people's differences will somehow infect or hurt us.

Unbecoming isn't easy. Some days I would much rather squeeze myself into a mold and stay there. That's when I remind myself that this work is not just about me. Although it starts with an inward focus and is often maligned as a selfish venture, unbecoming is one of the bravest things we can do. It causes ripples far beyond what we could ever imagine.

You see, the true work of changing the world isn't *out there* somewhere. Instead, it begins deep within ourselves. It requires that we peel back all the layers of expectation and fear and programming and discover our authentic selves—and then have the courage to share *that* person with the world.

# PART 3

# I EMBRACE BEAUTIFUL MESSINESS

What you most deeply long for is most likely within you right now. Maybe it's not our world that needs to change, but the way we show up in it. If we learn to look close enough, we'll discover there is beauty even in the world's cracks and crevices. These are reflections on being a beautiful, messy human.

# BOXES

I built a life of boxes. I devoted years to polishing and perfecting each one: professional speaker, family man, nonprofit leader. Achievements stacked up. I made goals and met them. Life was simple. I just didn't realize how much color it lacked.

The boxes made life manageable. They were dependable. I knew what would happen when I reached into each one. My speeches would be compelling. My family time would be wholesome. I would lead with wisdom and wit. I had it all under control.

Until I didn't.

A mounting sense of dissatisfaction festered within me. My days overflowed with tasks and obligations, people and demands. But all of my busyness only pushed contentment farther and farther away. Each accolade left me yearning for the next one. Satisfaction was always just out of reach. My boxes were full, but I was empty.

Something was missing. I rifled through the boxes again and again. Slowly at first, and then more frantically. Where was it? It had to be there. I had followed all of the rules. I had done everything right. I had crossed all the t's and dotted all the i's just like I was supposed to do. Yet I felt nothing.

"Where do you feel your feelings?"

My therapist's ridiculous question hung in the air. I looked at my six safe boxes. The answer wasn't there. My inner world held buttoned-up, smoothed-out boxes—not messy, unpredictable feelings.

So I laughed. And she waited patiently.

It would take many sessions before I could respond to her simple inquiry.

I used to turn to the boxes for comfort; now they just mocked me. Dread, disappointment, and a deep sorrow filled me as I realized my mistake. My inner world was beige, boring, brittle. Every surface was too slick, too smooth, too predictable. I craved a depth and authenticity that my boxes weren't made to hold.

My boxes were safe, not good. I had confused the two, thinking they were synonyms. As I journeyed through therapy, my inner world expanded. It turns out that the real magic of boxes is when you open them and get to see what's inside. You tear apart the old boxes to make way for new discoveries. Six boxes became sixteen became thirty-seven. I discovered new boxes—complex, confusing places inside of me with bright, garish colors I immediately wanted to hide away. This internal deconstruction was every bit as painful and devastating as building my boxes had been rewarding and easy.

"Why do I need to feel my feelings?"

My ridiculous question hung in the air. I looked at the tattered remains of my six safe boxes. They'd given me so much. I'm a nice guy. I have a great family. I run a successful business. So *what* if I was numb inside?

This time my therapist answered. And I listened. It would take many sessions before I could believe her response.

The truth is that we don't get to choose the beautiful without the messy. They're two sides of the same coin, two verses of the same song, two chords from the same guitar. Not feeling the hard stuff means we don't truly feel the good stuff either. We don't appreciate a great day until we've had a terrible one. There's no favorite meal without all the forgettable ones. And it's hard to be grateful for our health until we've been sick.

I had lived my whole life striving for happiness and running from sorrow, never imagining that I needed both. Slowly, I've been learning to embrace the entire range of human emotions. Anything less would be denying myself the full human experience. Feeling pain is the only way I will ever truly feel joy, let it sink down into my soul, and watch contentment bloom.

Sometimes I long for the one-note song of my old life, where I knew the rhythm and wasn't scared of an unexpected octave change. Then I hear a symphony, and it's like I'm hearing music for the first time. I'm stuck in my seat as it moves me to tears. It makes me feel. It makes me human. And I know I can never return to my six safe boxes again.

# LITTLE SPARKS OF GENEROSITY

When you have young kids, Halloween is a really big deal. The weeks (months?) leading up to the big day are filled with mounting candy expectations and endless costume debates. One day your kid wants to be Superman, and the next, they're telling you all the reasons why Batman is so much better. They change their minds a dozen times as they flit excitedly between the many options. Then they land on the same idea as their sibling and begin arguing about who thought of it first!

Even as adults, there's so much anticipation that comes with Halloween because it marks the beginning of the holiday season. The very next day is November, which means you are just weeks away from Thanksgiving, which is just a million shopping trips and holiday parties away from Christmas. It's like the first day of a grand vacation, and you just can't wait to experience everything in front of you.

As you can probably tell, my kids love Halloween, and I do too. When everyone is finally dressed in their carefully chosen, much-debated costume (a feat in itself with small children), we come together for the traditional candy-seeking walk around the neighborhood. We stroll along happily with all the other families, enjoying the spooky decorations and creative costumes. No door is left unknocked. No candy is left behind. The night is full of laughter, sugar, and togetherness.

I have one Halloween memory that stands out from the rest. My son Lincoln was two years old, and I was pulling him and our one-year-old neighbor in a wagon. We'd already visited quite a few houses and were getting close to finishing up for the night. Then I saw a group of three middle school boys, not a demographic overwhelmingly known for their maturity, good choices, or citizenship (I know I wasn't, at that age). They were hyped up on candy, dressed up in costumes, and whipped up into a frenzy of Halloween-fueled excitement. Oh boy.

They stuck out to me because there were no parents around them. I guessed that this was probably the first year they were trick-or-treating unsupervised. And I hoped they would celebrate with more treats than tricks. As we passed by, I told them how great their costumes looked. They smiled and kept going.

Then, when they were about twenty feet past us, one of them turned around. There was clearly something on his mind. He had seen the toddlers in the wagon, and some little spark of generosity had stirred within him. Without saying anything to his friends, he started walking back to us. He reached into his pillowcase, pulled out two pieces of candy, and dropped one each into the buckets sitting in the laps of the two little boys.

When his friends noticed what he had done, they also followed suit, each one placing a piece of their candy into each toddler's bucket. I thanked them and prompted my son to do the same. It was such a small moment, but it spoke loudly to me and has stuck with me for years.

I'm just so grateful that middle school boy listened to that little spark of generosity. He could have easily ignored it, as I've certainly done before. One of the greatest lies I've told myself is that if I can just do X, get through Y, and navigate past Z, then I will be in a place where I can be generous.

That line of thinking allows me to walk past, ignore, or brush off the needs of others while I wait for some elusive, perfect set of circumstances to make an impact on the world. It allows me to feel better about showing up in the world as someone who takes instead of gives. Even though the reality is that being generous here and now would cost me about as much as those two pieces of candy cost that middle school boy: nothing. He gave out of his excess, not even putting a dent in his haul.

That middle schooler also completely turned around (quite an analogy for many of us) to do something generous and thoughtful and kind. Surely, if that boy had weighed the decision, he would have found far more reasons to just keep walking. His actions took effort and involved risk. But he did it anyway, simply because it felt like the right thing to do. I have a lot to learn from him.

Those three boys often come to mind when the world seems overwhelmingly dark or unkind. It bolsters something inside of me to know that middle school boys who talk about farts all day long can experience little sparks of generosity and have the courage to respond to them. It fills me with hope to know that the very best of humanity exists even in awkward, moody adolescent boys. And if it's in them, then it's in all of us. The very best of ourselves, just waiting for us to listen.

# BEING HUMAN

Recently I was on a flight heading to an important meeting. I had activated my do-not-engage-people mode—noise-canceling headphones and an open laptop—and I was fully focused on my work.

Then the flight attendants brought the snacks. Out of the corner of my eye, I realized the elderly woman sitting next to me was having trouble opening her pretzels. I stopped typing long enough to silently gesture that I was willing to open them if she'd like. She handed them over, I opened them, and she mouthed "Thank you," with a big smile. A few minutes later came the drink cart. Out of the corner of her eye, she realized my laptop was covering my entire tray. She patted her tray table and whispered loudly, "You can put your drink on my tray." I sat my drink down and smiled in thanks.

That simple exchange stayed with me for weeks. I remember her shaky hands. I remember her smile. I remember how good it felt when she saw my need and offered to help. I remember the joy of connection.

We all crave deep human connections—to see and be seen, to serve and be served. That's what we were made for, but it often seems so out of reach. We think we're too busy or too overwhelmed or too incapable to forge deep friendships or make meaningful connections. So instead we do nothing.

But what if the bar is so much lower than we could imagine? What if the opportunity for human connection is all around us? What if it's as simple as pausing to see someone's small need and offer to help? What if it's as easy as leaving just enough margin in our lives to connect with the people around us?

I believe it is just that simple and easy. That shared moment of humanity on the flight was merely the most recent example in a long list of small human connections that have enriched, improved, and affirmed my life and my ability to touch the lives around me.

One of my favorite examples of the power of small human connections occurred when I was attending an event one night in Houston. The event required cash to park, and I had none on me, not a single dollar. So I went to get some gas a few blocks away and was just racking my brain for how I could solve the problem without having to drive around to find an ATM.

Just then, a car pulled up at the pump next to me. There were three young Black men in the car. The driver got out, looked around kind of awkwardly, and then asked me, "Is there no place to pay with cash?" I looked around. Sure enough, there were no workers or small kiosk to be found. It was a card-only station. By this time, my pump was finished, but I knew the solution to my problem had just arrived.

"Hey, man, I know it's weird," I said, "but I'll pay for your gas with my card if you give me the cash. I actually need it for parking at an event around the corner."

"Oh yeah, no problem," he answered. "I was just going to do thirty dollars."

I ran my card on his pump, he handed me the cash, and I started to get in my truck to leave. That's when the young man called out, "I promise I'll stop it at thirty."

"I trust you," I said. "Take care of yourself."

As I drove away, I wondered how often this young man had ever heard the words "I trust you" from an older man like me. By the way, I checked my credit card account online a few days afterward. He only used twenty-eight dollars.

Both of these interactions took mere seconds, but there's a reason that I'm still talking about them. These stories remind me what it means to be human. They are about showing up, extending trust, giving the benefit of the doubt, and choosing to see someone as simply another human being.

It's about laying aside, and not even caring about, all the demographic facts and figures that usually separate us, not knowing about the other person's politics, résumé, level of education, income bracket, number of speeding tickets, or how they treat their mom. We don't need to know any of those things. All we need is a willingness to show up and see each other. One tiny moment at a time.

# NEVER GROW UP

When people joke around about not wanting to grow up, they generally mean that they don't want to deal with adult responsibilities. They are tired of being burdened by the heaviness of the world and the weight of being a grown-up. I totally get it. I like Peter Pan as much as anyone.

But maybe there's a better reason for not wanting to grow up. Being grown up tends to make us less gracious, less generous, and less willing to respond when we see somebody in need. It's hard to see this shift as it occurs. We just slowly get more focused on ourselves, our goals, and our society's expectations. But if you spend any time around children, they'll remind you of how you used to be.

I remember one summer I was driving around town with my (then) young daughter Micah. It was the time of year when many of the college kids in our town were moving out of their rental homes. We were in one of the neighborhoods near campus when we saw a man digging through trash cans.

I honestly didn't think much of it, but seven-year-old Micah was deeply disturbed by the sight and asked why he was doing that. I explained that he was probably looking for food or something he could sell for food. That made her even more upset. Then I told her that college students sometimes throw away nice things and that he might uncover some useful items. Micah simply couldn't stomach the sight of this man looking through someone else's trash. This situation was unacceptable to her.

She immediately began searching for a solution, and I tried my best to stay out of her way:

"We should give him food," she said.

"We don't have any food," I said.

"We should give him money to buy food."

"I'm not sure I have any cash, sweetie."

"I saw some in the cupholder," she pointed out.

"You are right, dear. Take it. Go and give it to him," I told her.

Micah jumped out of the car and walked purposefully toward the man. I hung back so he wouldn't feel overwhelmed. I heard Micah tell him that she was sorry he was digging through the trash. Then she held out the money, explaining that she got it from her dad and that she hoped he would use it to buy something nice for himself. The man looked shocked. He talked to her for a while, but I couldn't quite hear him. Then I saw her give him a side hug and march back toward me.

When she returned to the car, she reported that he was looking for items to clean up and sell and that no one had ever stopped to give him money. Micah also commented that he was very nice, and she thought it was so great that he was finding a way to earn money to take care of himself. As we drove away, she remarked that it was sad that his bank account probably didn't have very much money in it.

I was proud of my daughter but also a bit surprised at what this encounter revealed about me. I know that I wouldn't have responded in the same way if I had been alone in the car. I probably would have ignored that man. If the thought of giving him money even crossed my mind, I would've weighed out all the cultural layers of nuance and uncertainty involved in such a situation: The man could have been dangerous. I didn't know what he would do with the money. Maybe he would be insulted that I was trying to give him a handout.

Those are very real possibilities, but Micah's response was clearly the better option. She led with kindness and didn't let worries about what might happen prevent her from being a force of good in the world.

So the next time I hear someone say that growing up is overrated, I will wholeheartedly agree. But the problem isn't taxes or job responsibilities or dealing with an aging body. The problem is how we let fear and laziness and cultural expectations hold us back from giving generously to others. Thankfully, it's not an insurmountable problem. Our children will show us how to get back to the wisdom we once knew. It's still inside of us—we just have to get out of our own way sometimes.

# MR. BURGER'S GIFT

Micah came home from preschool one day, chattering away about the wonders of recycling. When I explained that our neighborhood didn't actually have a recycling program, a look of steely determination came over her. Never one to let problems stand in her way, Micah decided that she would start her own recycling business.

After spreading the word with flyers and knocking on doors, five-year-old Micah had about fifteen families in our neighborhood signed up for her new ten-dollars-a-month recycling pickup service. Pretty soon, she and I had a new routine of driving around the neighborhood every Thursday morning before school, rain or shine, to pick up people's glass, aluminum, and cardboard items and take them to the local recycling center. That's where we met Mr. Burger.

Mr. Burger was a retirement-aged Latino man who worked at the recycling center. Every week, he helped us unload everyone's recycling from the back of our truck. But he didn't just do his job and go on his way. Instead, he always seemed genuinely happy to see us and took the time to stop and visit with us. And over the following weeks and months, he became an important part of our lives.

One of my favorite Mr. Burger moments happened the day after Micah's sixth birthday. Like most little kids, she was super excited to tell all her friends about this big event in her life. And, of course, that included Mr. Burger. I'd been hearing her tell people about her birthday all week. Most adults responded with "I hope you have a great birthday!" or "Are you going to have a party?" They threw out the appropriate words to keep moving the conversation forward, just like I usually do.

Not so for Mr. Burger. His response wasn't a statement or a question: it was an action. As soon as Micah told him about her birthday, he reached into his pocket and handed her four dollars. The only money he had on him. This elderly man who worked at a recycling center handed my child his last dollar. I immediately teared up as I considered his willingness to risk loving well and fully and at a cost to himself.

His knee-jerk, gut-level response to give instead of holding back reminded me of a Bible story I grew up hearing. It's about a widow who gives her last two coins to the church. The first time I heard that story, it was probably acted out on a flannel board while I sipped watered-down Kool-Aid at Vacation Bible School. But soon enough, I could recite the story from memory. And every single time I did, I imagined myself as the generous widow.

I was used to being at the center of the story. I was used to being the one praised for his generosity. I was used to being on the power side of the giving equation. And, honestly, I liked the power and control and praise that afforded me. Being on the receiving end felt weird and wrong. It made me feel weak and vulnerable and even a little embarrassed. But it also taught me a lot.

Something about Mr. Burger's generosity really challenged me. When people ask me for money, a whole bunch of questions run through my head: What will they spend it on? Do they really need this? Will I still have enough for me? Mr. Burger didn't do any of that. He bypassed all the hemming and hawing and jumped immediately to the giving. While I would have still been asking dumb questions in my head, he was already handing over his money. I want to be more like Mr. Burger.

I had never imagined that a first-generation Hispanic man who works with trash all day would have so much to teach me about life. I had looked at his outward appearance and his humble job and underestimated him. I usually chose my mentors based on their financial success, impressive awards, and shiny lives. I would never have looked for a mentor in a trash pit. What a foolish mistake.

Yet it's a mistake that I see people make a lot, even people who read Jesus's words about the last being first, and judging not, and the value of humility. Just look at who's on most church leadership boards. They're usually people who are the most successful in business. I don't know a lot of churches with sanitation workers on church leadership. It's not that men working the trash trucks aren't full of the fruit of the Spirit. It's that we have a very skewed definition of success and a limited view of leadership.

My friendship with Mr. Burger changed me. I could probably fill a whole book (*Thursdays with Mr. Burger*) with the lessons he taught me about generosity and kindness and the dignity of work. He helped me understand the fruits of the Spirit in ways that no sermon ever had.

All in all, Recycling with Micah went on for over two years, kept about 14,000 pounds of trash from the landfill, and allowed her to save enough money for a semester of college. But some of my most precious memories from that season of our lives were from the unexpected, unlikely, and uncommon friendship we forged with Mr. Burger.

# MR. BURGER PART II

Almost exactly a year after Mr. Burger's generous gift to Micah, we received an extraordinary opportunity to match his graciousness.

When we dropped off the recycling one Thursday morning, I checked in with him and asked how his family was doing. He shared that his wife was going to have surgery on her eyes. After the procedure, she wouldn't be able to drive, work, or even be on the computer. She was going to be out of commission for several weeks. I knew from previous conversations that she was an hourly employee, so I knew she wouldn't have sick leave to cover her time off.

I asked Mr. Burger if there was anything we could do to help. He said that he would appreciate our prayers. I assured him that we would pray, then asked if there were any other ways we could serve him. When he seemed reluctant to answer, I reassured him that he was our friend and that we really, truly did want to help.

He finally said, "Well, sometimes we like to make tamales. Maybe you could help me sell some tamales to cover the deductible for her surgery." Yes! I was honored that he trusted me enough to allow me to come alongside him during a difficult time in his life. He believed me when I told him that he didn't have to go through it alone. Just as he had accompanied us and helped us, I was grateful for the opportunity to do the same.

And I knew exactly how to sell those tamales. I had already shared about Mr. Burger a number of times online. Whenever his overwhelming generosity struck me or moved me, I would post about it on social media. He was enriching my life and Micah's life, and I hoped that others would feel the benefit as well.

So I decided to put up another Mr. Burger post. I believe people want to help when they can. When they're given clear opportunities to help, they will. I went home and explained the situation on my Facebook page, hoping to sell about 50 dozen tamales.

Of course, once I told (then seven-year-old) Micah what I had done, she immediately one-upped me and asked to add her own message to the post:

> "Mr. Burger is very sweet, and his tamales are very good. Generosity is very important because his wife had surgery, so he wants to help her with this. I hope we sell 70 dozen of them."

I started by asking for 50 dozen tamales, Micah upped it to 70 dozen, and within an hour or so, we had sold over 100 dozen tamales! We tried to cap it there, but somehow we ended up selling a total of 113 dozen tamales. Mr. Burger's generosity sparked generosity in others. It was a beautiful thing to witness.

Most of my Facebook friends had never even met Mr. Burger. If it weren't for Micah's recycling business, I wouldn't have either. These kinds of friendships don't happen naturally. My natural inclination is to surround myself with people who look like me, think like me, and are in my tax bracket. I have to make conscious choices to connect with people outside of my circle. I have to be intentional if I don't want to lead an insulated life.

I'm a fairly outgoing, gregarious person, but it's still easier for me to relate to people who know my lingo and understand my worldview than to stretch myself to connect with people who are different from me. But taking the easier way out only led me to the realization that I could go for days, weeks, and even months at a time without interacting in a meaningful way with anyone who saw or experienced the world differently than me. Mr. Burger saved me from that.

These kinds of friendships also aren't formed by mere proximity. I could have easily just dropped off my recycling, patted myself on the back, and drove away. Most days, I had a mile-long to-do list waiting for me, so I could have easily justified skating through my interactions with Mr. Burger as quickly as possible. Thankfully, Micah and Mr. Burger wouldn't let me get away with that. She wanted to chat and say hi and make a friend. And he was more than willing to oblige.

Mr. Burger and I built a relationship slowly over many Thursdays and alongside many cardboard pizza boxes, aluminum soda cans, and plastic milk cartons. Small, consistent encounters led to a big, beautiful friendship. Some of the richest, best parts of life come from those sorts of seemingly inconsequential actions. When enough people take enough small, good actions, beautiful changes can occur. That kind of beauty is all around us. Sometimes it's camouflaged as an unlikely friendship, and other times it looks like helping sell tamales for ten dollars a dozen, but it's definitely out there. I hope I always have eyes to see it.

# MONEY

So much of who we want to be as adults involves returning to who we were as kids. We might have been more human back then. We want to laugh and enjoy life, so we need to remember how to play. We want more, better, deeper friendships, so we need to start inviting people over for playdates. We want to be kinder and gentler, so we need to open our tightly closed fists.

Some of the very best versions of ourselves are those five-, six-, seven-, or eight-year-old selves that we left behind years ago. You can say a lot about those kids' naivete and lack of understanding about how the world works. You can make fun of their poor fashion choices and wonder how they convinced their mothers to let them leave the house like that. But I don't think it's an accident that Jesus said the Kingdom of God belongs to those who are like children.

Somewhere along the way, social pressure squeezes out some of the very best of us. We give up what we know in our guts to be true so we can fit in. One of the starkest examples of this is in our relationship with money. Thankfully, we have our children to lead us. They can show us how to reclaim our generosity and kindness. Our kids will teach us if we just move out of the way. At least, that's how it seems to happen in my life.

One day I took then five-year-old Micah and four-year-old Beckett to get our minivan washed. For a while, they were entertained by the whir of the car wash and the sight of suds flying, but they grew a bit antsy waiting for everything to finish up. So I decided to let them buy something cool to drink from a vending machine. We sat in the shade, enjoying our sodas and watching three men dry the van. The workers' shirts were soaked with sweat, and they were in perpetual motion, making sure the van was sparkling clean.

That's when I reached into my wallet and immediately realized my conundrum. I didn't have any dollar bills on me. The only cash I had was a single ten-dollar bill. The problem was that I didn't want to tip ten dollars. I only wanted to tip a couple of bucks like I normally did. The whole car wash was only a little over ten dollars. I didn't want to double it! Should I tip too much or not at all? That was the question. I decided to punt this difficult decision to my kids.

I turned to Micah and Beckett and said, "Guys, I need your help with something. When the workers finish with the car, we usually give them one or two dollars. But I only have ten dollars. That's kind of a lot of money for drying a car. What do you think we should do?"

They didn't even hesitate. They didn't need any time to consider the options or weigh the ramifications. "Give it to them," Micah said. "They've been working hard, and it's hot out here."

"Yeah," Beckett said. "Give it to them." Then they both looked at me like I was crazy, since I was clearly worried about nothing. I could almost see them thinking, *We're watching these guys sweat and work hard to clean our car while we're sitting in the shade sipping sodas. Why are we even talking about this? Give them the money.*

So I did. Or, actually, I let the kids do the honors. It was their idea after all. Micah and Beckett had huge grins on their faces as they handed over the ten-dollar bill. The men were surprised and grateful. And I was reminded, yet again, about the power of viewing the world through the eyes of a child.

My kids showed me that something needed to change about my relationship with money. I had grown up at times with a scarcity mentality—we had a big family, and my parents purposely took jobs that prioritized family time over salary. So we always had enough but not always a lot of extra. That idea about money persisted when I was a young pastor and my wife stayed at home with our children. And, of course, running a nonprofit meant I was always focused on raising more and more money. So giving away ten dollars felt like such a big deal because money itself was a big deal.

I had never paused long enough to evaluate my relationship with money and see if it was still serving me. That became painfully obvious when some of my side hustles became successful and my income started rising. Suddenly, I had plenty of money, but I continued feeling like it was never enough. I realized that I needed to put in some hard work around my relationship with money and look at how it was contributing to or holding me back from the person I wanted to be.

We all have stories we tell ourselves about money. And, if you're like me, it's a story you'll need to keep evaluating and modifying as your life grows and changes. Most people get weird about money at some point, but thankfully, kids aren't weird about money. They're generous with it. They give it away freely. They're foolish enough to believe in the goodness of sharing. Our kids will help us rewrite our money stories and lead the way in kindness and generosity if we will let them. I'm sure of it.

# CHRISTMAS EVE PROSTITUTE

One Christmas Eve before we had kids, Stacey and I were trying to figure out how to commemorate what Jesus's birth is truly all about. There's a scandal to Christmas that we often forget: an unplanned baby born in an unwashed stable to an unwed couple. We wanted to honor that by doing something unexpected.

At this point in our lives, we had a lot of experience doing urban ministry and working with low-income families. It was something we felt very tender toward, and we wanted our unexpected action to make a meaningful difference in the life of at least one low-income family. But the Angel Tree thing just wasn't doing it for us that year.

As we tossed around ideas, we kept circling back to an area of town most people actively avoided, especially churchgoers. (And I should know because I was working as a youth pastor at that time.) It was an area deeply affected by drugs, crime, and prostitution.

We knew children of prostitutes. We knew women who provided for their children by whatever means necessary. We knew this was the reality of life for some of the families we loved and served. And we knew that's where we wanted to be on the eve of this celebration of the world's most remarkable scandal.

So we went to an ATM first and then drove to that well-known area where well-meaning folks rarely ventured. It was a chilly December night. The women waiting on the sidewalks must have been freezing. Our car pulled up, and a woman walked toward us. She was probably in her thirties. I rolled down the window, and she looked pretty surprised to see Stacey in the front seat.

Before she could speak, I held the cash out to her. Slowly, cautiously, she reached out her hand. I put the money in her palm and folded her fingers on top of it. "I hope you can go home now and be with your kids tonight," I said. And then we drove away.

I don't know what happened after that moment. I don't know if she went home. I don't know her story. I'd like to think that she still remembers that night. Not that she remembers us but that she remembers someone showed up and saw her in a vulnerable moment and didn't chastise her, berate her, preach at her, or use her for their own gain, but rather spoke into a part of her life that very few people had spoken into for a long time. The part that saw her as a mom and a person worthy of being loved.

Most of my adult life, I've focused on creating sustainable charity work that moves people out of vicious cycles of poverty. So I know that wasn't the most efficient, long-lasting, getting-at-the-root-cause donation that I've ever given. I surely didn't get a tax write-off for giving money to a prostitute! But it was one of my most meaningful, philanthropic moments of giving—mostly *because* it wasn't any of those things.

Sometimes those of us who value efficiency and scale and root-cause solutions can lose sight of what it means to meet face-to-face with another human being without theories or programs or five-step plans to insulate us from their need. It also changes the dynamic when we interact with someone knowing that we have no control over the outcome. That sort of giving forces us to remember what matters most and why we wanted to give in the first place.

I often like to spend Christmas thinking about what the day before Jesus's birth must have been like for Mary and Joseph. The shame of their out-of-wedlock pregnancy hanging over their heads with harsh words from unbelieving friends ringing in their ears. They were probably tired and bickering after a long journey and a few inevitable wrong turns. Plus, they were low on cash, couldn't find a place to stay, and had to sleep in a barn.

Christmas is the day for the underdog, the forgotten, the scandalized, the poor and lowly, and those without a place at the inn. The scandal of Christmas is the unexpected gift of love found in unexpected places. That's the miracle I celebrate and long for and try imperfectly to usher in.

The Christmas that we gave money to the prostitute felt holy in a way that a lot of other Christmas activities, even some very spiritual ones, haven't always made me feel. I felt connected to the scandal of Christmas in a new way. I wish I could say that this is a Christmas tradition that I've carried with me all these years, but I've never done that again. I need to spend some time thinking about why that might be.

# THE QUESTION

If you've ever been told to push forward and never look back, that is some of the worst advice you've ever been given. It's well intended, and I understand the sentiment, but it will likely only make you feel frustrated and dissatisfied with your life. Let me explain.

When we only look at where we want to go, we're staring at obstacles all the time. Our goals seem so far away, and there's a lot of hard work in front of us. Even if we're waking up early, going to bed late, and packing the hours in between, it never seems like enough. It's easy to get overwhelmed or discouraged because the goal is always just a little farther ahead.

As we continue focusing forward, we invariably grow more and more restless with *where we are* because we're so laser-focused on *where we want to be*. Right now is never good enough. We're not satisfied with what we have because all we see is what we lack. No matter how good things are in the present moment, all we can think about is how much better they'll be in the future.

So we continue believing the lie that the next few steps will finally satisfy us. But we keep taking steps forward, and we keep feeling dissatisfied. It's an endless, agonizing loop. It can leave us feeling broken and bruised and wondering if there is something horribly wrong with us. Thankfully, there's a way to break the cycle. I'll show you how it works.

One day, I asked my friend about his new business. He answered, "It's going pretty well, but...." Then he listed out all his big goals and all the work he still needed and wanted to do. There was nothing wrong with his answer. It was honest and real. But it made me sad. Here was a man living his dream of owning his own business, making more than enough to support his family, and doing an amazing job. But he still wasn't satisfied. I understood where he was coming from, though, because it's a road I've walked most of my professional life.

So I asked him a different question: "If you could rewind back to the day you started your business and see where you are today, how would you feel about your progress so far?"

His face immediately lit up. "One-year-ago-me wouldn't believe how great it's going right now." A second earlier, he had been frustrated about how far he had to go, and now he was celebrating how far he had come. Boom!

This question unlocks something in people, giving them permission to be proud of their progress and satisfied with their present reality. So I've started asking everyone this question: "What would your former self think about where you are today?" The most common response I hear is "That person wouldn't believe it if I told them." What a gift! But it's a gift we have to slow down in order to receive. Otherwise, it's wasted as we blow right past it.

I wish someone had asked me this question years ago when I was forever pushing and fighting, setting the bar higher and higher, and turning the speed up faster and faster on the treadmill. I was so laser-focused on where I needed to go that I lost sight of both where

I was and where I had been. It took a long time to unlearn those tendencies and find a healthier balance between forward momentum, past gratitude, and present contentment. In all honesty, it's something I'm still trying to do better. And this single question has been the biggest help in my growth to get there.

Contrary to that terrible advice you got all those years ago, looking back hasn't made me less motivated to keep growing and evolving. I still love the game. I still love the chase. I still love how it feels to win. I still believe in setting goals. But now that I'm not hyperfocused on my forward quest, I can also simultaneously feel more satisfied with who I am and where I am today. The ultimate win-win.

So let me ask you: "What would your former self think about where you are today?" If your answer is "They wouldn't freakin' believe it," then appreciate yourself. Let that gratitude and amazement fuel your next steps. Let that remind you that you've traveled hard journeys before, and you can do it again. Let yourself look back in order to make both today and the journey forward more joyful and fulfilling.

# AIRPORT CONNECTIONS

Something cool happened last week. It was a simple moment that lasted only a few minutes. It wasn't newsworthy or even particularly exciting. But it was one of the most meaningful experiences I've had in a long time.

The setting was the airport terminal. Boarding had just started. There was a big crowd at the gate. Everyone was on edge. Mothers wrangled small children, businessmen gripped their briefcases, and teenagers fired off one last text. You know the scene.

Then there was a commotion at the gate, and the steady flow of passengers suddenly came to a complete stop. I craned my neck to see what was going on and why the gate agents were speaking so loudly and slowly.

A Hispanic woman was standing at the gate with her young son. There was a problem with her ticket. She only spoke Spanish. The gate agents did not. They asked for any Spanish speakers to come forward, and someone from the back of the line stepped up to help. The Hispanic woman, the volunteer, and one of the gate agents stepped to the side to discuss the issue. The other gate agent restarted the boarding process.

As I got close to the front of the line, I heard the gate agent tell the volunteer that her bag would have to be checked at the gate if she stayed to help. The volunteer explained this wouldn't work because she had a very tight connection with no time to stop in baggage claim before her next flight. She asked to go set her bag down in the plane and then come back to translate. The gate agent told her that wasn't possible. The Spanish-speaking woman looked worried.

The solution seemed simple enough. I offered to take the volunteer's bag. My bag-carrying ability is better than my Spanish. It felt like the least I could do. "Row 7," the volunteer said, "and thank you." The Spanish-speaking woman looked relieved.

So there I was, pulling two carry-ons down the ramp to the plane—mine and the volunteer's. It was fine but a bit clunky. Then a college kid behind me said, "Let me grab that extra one for you. Row 7, right?"

"Yes," I said, "and thank you."

That's the way the world can be if only we will let it. I started by pulling the extra bag. The college student happily jumped in to help. The volunteer made her next flight. The Spanish-speaking woman got the help she needed and boarded a few minutes later. Four random people. Connected by four simple actions. Four days improved by simple gestures of compassion and kindness. And to think I could've missed it all.

I think of all the times I've missed similar opportunities. So often, I go through life with my head down and my mind elsewhere. I'm focused on my own problems and plans. I may even have headphones on or be absorbed in a great book. I put up so many barricades between me and the world around me. It's safer and easier and more comfortable to stay in my own little bubble. I can control everything in there. I don't have to worry about anyone else's needs or demands. That's nice for a while, but then the loneliness sets in.

It's impossible to imagine how many times I've sheltered myself away and missed other opportunities for meaningful connections. How many times I missed the chance to be human with other humans. To connect authentically with a stranger or three over a shared moment. Those moments may be inconvenient or awkward, but they fill my cup in a way that I deeply need and desperately crave.

The only way to break out of my bubble is to open myself to the present moment and start paying attention. At the airport, I was fully there, fully aware, fully open to connecting with others. If you're like me, that doesn't happen naturally. It takes intention to show up fully in the present moment. But man, the payoffs are huge.

Being fully aware opens us up to moments of deep human connection. And when that connection occurs between strangers, it is so powerful. We often think of that connection between strangers in stories like the passengers on Flight 93 who fought back against the terrorists, or a story about a group of people who formed a human rope to pull someone out of a river. When people open themselves to others, it's true that big and amazing things can happen.

Maybe I can be part of something that big and grand one day. That would be awesome. But those are once-in-a-lifetime types of situations. It's much more common that I'm going to see a stranger crying or a stray dog roaming the neighborhood or a frazzled mom with more screaming babies than hands. Or two women speaking a shared language, both just trying to get home. Each of those is an opportunity to step in and connect with another living creature on a deep, meaningful level. Those small moments may not get the press or go viral, but the depth of connection is just as significant. I hope I don't miss too many more of them.

# 5,000 PIECES OF PIZZA

There is a lot of chatter about our culture being on the brink of a mental health crisis. Everywhere we turn, we hear buzzwords about psychology and self-care. More and more people are talking about going to therapy, and the use of psychiatric medications is on the rise. And there are heated debates over whether this is a positive or negative development.

Some people say that the increased awareness around mental health is a sign of people being soft. They contrast this generation with how strong people were "back in the day." Maybe if we all toughened up and no one got a participation trophy, we wouldn't have to hear about all of this mental health stuff. Others say this breakdown is long overdue. We've neglected our mental health for far too long. It's not that people weren't anxious or depressed in the past; it's that they weren't willing to acknowledge or share about it.

As with most debates, it's not as simple as either of those two options. But I think the real problem is that we're debating the wrong thing. We're not talking enough about the external factors causing this cultural shift toward poor mental health.

Our world is vastly different than it used to be. There are obvious advancements that have allowed us to go faster, be more efficient, harness the power of technology, and on and on. It's a minor miracle that we can use our voices to get any question answered instantaneously. That's straight out of *The Jetsons*. We gush about having the entire world at our fingertips, but maybe we should be lamenting the pain and weight and burden that comes with having the entire world at our fingertips.

A postal worker in Missouri can google and find videos of children working in the coal mines in Venezuela. A mother, up in the middle of the night nursing her newborn in Dallas, Texas, can read hundreds of news articles and even find video of a mass shooting that just happened across the country. Not only can she read the original story, but she can hear the voices and read the reactions of hundreds or even thousands of other people, amplifying the entire situation in a worldwide echo chamber.

Guys, no one prepared us for this! In past generations, people would read a sad story in their local paper, or the evening news might spend three minutes touching on a nearby tragedy, and if someone was very noble-minded, they might subscribe to the *New York Times* or *National Geographic* for snippets of meaningful stories from around the world. Bad news was never instantaneous, was always in 2D, and was rarely the only type of story you would read. Every bad story would be surrounded by feel-good stories to soften the reality of the really hard stuff you were reading.

We are digesting more bad news every day than we could ever possibly process. Yet we seem surprised that our emotional capacity and mental health haven't been able to keep up. It's like being surprised that the human body cannot suddenly eat 5,000 pieces of pizza in a day. You know that if you try to eat that many pieces of pizza in a day, your body would literally force you to stop. And so it seems our hearts and minds are trying to do the same.

It is amazing that we have access to the information that we do. It is also crushing many of us from the inside out. Empathetic people take the pain of each news story directly onto their shoulders, welcome it into their hearts, and hold it deeply in their souls. Then there are people like me who hear about a problem and immediately go into strategy mode. My heart and soul remain shut down and sealed off. I don't feel other people's pain; I just try to fix it. Neither approach is healthy or sustainable in the long run. They'll bring equal amounts of pain, just on different schedules.

I don't think the solution is to care less. I do think the solution might involve a lot more intentionality in how we curate our newsfeeds. We throw the term "screen time" around, and for most of us, the idea is that there's something about the electronic connection that could be doing harm. But what if the real damage is what those screens are doing to our hearts and minds and our capacity for hope?

If we grieved every tragedy we came across with the depth that each of them certainly deserves, we would never change out of our funeral clothes. We would need a lifetime supply of Tylenol for the crying-induced headaches we would all experience twenty-four hours a day. The results would be cataclysmic, affecting every area of our lives. Nobody could possibly live like that.

Tonight, I'll coach my eight-year-old's machine-pitch baseball game. It's an important one. We are just a few games away from the end of the season and tied for first place. My favorite part of coaching his team is that for six innings, there will be no bad news. I will spend every moment of that entire block of time encouraging, cheering, and teaching a field full of seven- and eight-year-olds little lessons that are as much about life as they are about baseball. After an hour or so, someone will win and someone will lose.

But every kid on the field will smile at some point, if not throughout the entire game.

This isn't to minimize the pain and suffering of others. In fact, just yesterday, I read a post from a friend whose eighteen-year-old daughter with a rare genetic disorder died suddenly. That family feels pinned to the ground by the weight of their current grief. It is very real. It is very sad. And it is worth mourning, not for days but for many months and years to come. And yet, the death of that young girl is such a powerful reminder not to miss the moments of real life happening among us every day.

So we're left striving for this elusive balance: acknowledging the huge tragedies happening in the world while appreciating the small blessings occurring all around us. I'm not sure how to do that well, but I think it likely starts with acknowledging that there's too much pizza on my plate, more than I could ever eat.

# UNTIL I DIE

When I was a youth pastor, I used to tell the kids, "There's someone in your school who will go an entire day without anyone speaking to them. If that isn't you, be grateful. Then try to find that person. Talk with them, get to know them, and be their friend. No one should be alone." It was a good lesson for teens and tweens. It's a pretty good lesson for adults, too.

The older I get, the sadder I feel about people who are alone. There are children without families and women who birth babies without a hand to hold. There are people who die alone in hospital beds with no family or friends gathered around them. Some people don't even have a funeral. No one writes them an obituary or shows up by their casket or stands up to say a few kind words about them. Just think about how awful that is.

Being completely and utterly alone is one of the bleakest outcomes I can imagine. Maybe that's why I feel so uncomfortable in nursing homes. It is a place full of people at the end of their lives, all alone. It is a place where vulnerability and lack of control often show up as uninvited guests. It is a place full of people like Kevin.

I met Kevin one holiday season when my family visited a local nursing home to deliver flowers and Little Debbie snacks. The kids were great. Generous with their hugs and their "Merry Christmas" wishes. As we were walking out the front door, we noticed a man in a wheelchair all alone on the front porch. His name was Kevin. He had throat cancer. And he had been there for two months. After a few minutes of small talk, we shared this exchange:

> "How long do you think you'll be here?"
>
> "Until I die," he said, looking at the sky.
>
> He later told me his doctor estimated that time would come sometime in the next nine months.

Kevin had no family. None. He was as alone as you can be. He spent his days reading books from the "library" that consisted of three shelves of old novels. I promised to bring him more books and even take him to a bookstore to choose his own. He seemed grateful but rather neutral. Maybe that's what happens when you're alone—you get used to being disappointed.

When I left the nursing home that day, I was stirred up and deeply moved. I posted Kevin's story on social media, ending with this encouragement: "Life is short, friends. No one should be alone. Let's slow down and see each other. Let's go to those uncomfortable places. Let's give our lives away. Let's love well. For all the Kevins out there." I felt pretty good about that sign-off, the way I wrapped up a difficult situation with a neat bow and a strong call to action.

But then someone commented that they knew Kevin. He had painted their home several years before. My neat little bow quickly unraveled. I had been viewing Kevin through the lens of pity and need and helplessness. That made him separate from me. It allowed me to keep his pain at a distance. I could help Kevin, but I would never become Kevin. Now all that had shattered.

He wasn't just "Kevin who would die alone of throat cancer." He was Kevin who used to be healthy and strong and entrepreneurial enough to start a house-painting business. Just like I am healthy and strong and entrepreneurial enough to start my own businesses. *Oh shit*, I thought. *I really could become Kevin. I could live a full life and still end up alone.*

Surely Kevin never planned on his life ending this way. Surely he lived and worked and made friends and had a family and loved people and was loved by people. He probably hurt people and was hurt by people, too. His life before I met him was probably like most of our lives, a mix of beautiful and messy.

So what was the one problem, the one misstep, the one horrible day that led him to that nursing home where he waited for death all alone? *Maybe if I discovered Kevin's fateful mistake, I could stop myself from making it*, I thought. But it doesn't work that way. We can't prevent our worst nightmares from happening. Preparation and planning can only take us so far.

The truth is that I could end up alone. It's terrifying to think about. It makes my hands sweat and my muscles tighten and my heart beat faster. But there's nowhere for all that anxious energy to go. I can't solve this problem because it doesn't yet exist.

All that I can do is reach out to the real people facing real aloneness right now. These are the people who will go an entire day without anyone speaking to them. I've already found one of those people. I think it's about time for me to visit him again. Not out of pity but out of a deep sense of our shared humanity and an unshakable conviction that no one should be alone.

# SORRY

One night, I was rocking my then two-year-old son Lincoln to sleep when he accidentally banged his head into mine. My sweet boy immediately said, "Sorry, Daddy. Sorry, Daddy," before grabbing my face and kissing me on the lips. He did this three times in a row before I could even tell him it was okay. I couldn't help but think: *Oh, what a world it would be if we were all so quick to say "Sorry" when we messed up.*

I suck at saying I'm sorry. Instead, I act like apologizing will somehow make me more wrong, as if admitting my mistake will amplify it. I tell myself this story: *Maybe the person will just forget, or maybe they didn't notice, or maybe I'm making too big of a deal out of it.* That line of thinking keeps me quiet, hoping the whole thing will just go away—even though I know better.

Even if I move past those barriers and actually want to reach out and apologize, shame will usually hold me back. But any time that shame takes the driver's seat, whatever happens next is bound to be bad. Shame steers me through feelings of humiliation, reminds me of past traumas, and tries to convince me that I am fatally flawed and unworthy of forgiveness. Shame has never taken me to a good place. I know that for a fact.

Sometimes I don't apologize out of shame. Sometimes I don't apologize out of pride. When pride gets ahold of me, it tries to convince me to give the non-apology apology. You know the one: "I'm sorry you were offended by what I said." This kind of "apology" bears no blame, takes no credit, and acknowledges no wrong. It's actually worse than saying nothing at all. Anyone in a serious relationship knows that the non-apology apology is like a hand grenade escalating a disagreement into an all-out war.

But at two years old, Lincoln didn't have shame or pride holding him back. He had yet to learn about the non-apology apology. He just knew that he had hurt his dad, and he felt bad about it. He didn't qualify or justify or explain away the pain he had caused. He simply said, "I'm sorry." And you could tell he really meant it.

When I hurt someone, I wish my first thought was to let them know that I am sorry. I wish I didn't have to push past my shame-based attempts at self-preservation or my pride's insistence that I validate or minimize my mistake. I wish I didn't immediately go into fix-it mode to attempt to justify or explain away my error. How much richer my life would be if my immediate gut response was just to say I'm sorry.

I want to apologize freely and easily. I want to be big enough to admit mistakes. But in my lack of comfort with who I am, I let what should be a really simple response become much more complicated. And this just perpetuates and accentuates the mistake, causing more pain to the person I wronged and weighing me down with even more guilt and shame.

I wholeheartedly agree with the Roman philosopher Seneca, who said, "We suffer more often in imagination than in reality." We imagine that apologizing will draw attention to our mistake and tarnish our reputation. We think it will make everything worse.

In reality, we're just as wrong without an apology as we are with one—actually much more so because we're doubling down on being wrong.

Refusing to apologize hurts us, too. When we don't apologize, we carry a weight of obligation. We know that we owe the other person something, and that realization clouds the entire relationship. We feel perpetually indebted to them. And the crazy thing is that we have the ability to pay off that debt. There is money in our bank account; we're just refusing to pay. The creditors are calling every day, and we keep insisting that they have the wrong number.

Those creditors don't have to call. We have the means to alleviate the pain. I know I have the capacity to say I'm sorry when I hurt someone. I just have to have the guts to actually do it.

# FATHERING

When my children were younger, I used to take them to the grocery store, wearing one in an infant carrier, pushing one in the cart, and having the other two walk beside me. Every time I did this, people would smile and say, "Good job!" But when my wife did exactly the same thing, she got virtually none of those same responses.

The double standard is infuriating. It's like society gives dads a parenting pass. Their only role is to make babies and pay for babies' stuff. Their partner can do everything else. Dads are the financial providers while moms are the emotional, spiritual, hold-the-house-together providers. So any time a dad is actually parenting his children, it seems remarkable.

I know the people who praise me in the grocery store are trying to be nice. But no matter what actually comes out of their mouths, I interpret every seemingly supportive comment as "Whoa, you were willing to leave the house by yourself with little kids *and* you're keeping them all alive." That can't be our standard for fatherhood.

My wife and I feel equally called and equipped to take care of our children. Maybe we have a different style, and maybe there are more dad jokes and pieces of candy involved, but the bar for me is not keeping my kids alive. The bar is creating the same depth of emotional connection and presence as my wife provides. Yes, it looks and feels different because we are not the same people, but it's not because of our genders.

Yet no matter how many men I know who actually parent their children, almost every TV sitcom tells a different story. Dads on TV are shown as being so oblivious. They're too focused on the big game to see their kid sneaking out of the house. Or they're so focused on grilling hamburgers (the one culturally appropriate form of male cooking) that they don't realize the house is on fire. There's this ridiculous pop-culture narrative that dads are bumbling idiots who can hardly take care of themselves, much less their kids.

The problem is that if you tell a story long enough, people begin to believe it's true. Men will live into the expectations culture has for them. They might even embrace the story. And since the bar has been set so low and for so long, they might even think they should be praised when they meet that low bar.

We claim gender equality, but expectations placed on fathers are so unbelievably low. We laud fathers for simply doing their jobs. This double standard has shown up over and over in my life. My wife, her mom, and her sister have gone away for a girls' weekend once a year for the last decade. Every time they do, someone will comment on how incredible it is that I would take care of my own children. It's considered this minor miracle that I keep them alive and don't burn the house down. Yet I travel frequently for work, and my wife is never praised for being alone with the kids.

We've got to do better. We can't set the bar so low that we're surprised when we see a dad at the store with his kids. We have to raise it so that it's considered normal for a dad to watch his kids when his wife goes away. The only way this will change is if dads insist the bar be raised, even if that means they have to dig deeper than they're used to digging. And this is an open invitation for moms to start expecting and demanding more of their male partners. My wife has done that plenty. I didn't always like it, but I almost always needed it.

Fathering isn't easy work, but it is work worth fighting for. My life is richer, messier, and more beautiful as a fully engaged father than it could ever be if I kept my kids at arm's length. There has to be a generational shift away from the mentality that men aren't able to take care of their children. We need a generation of dads who take the low bar of fatherhood and declare that it is not good enough.

# OUR COLLECTIVE CAPACITY

During the 2020 presidential election, after reading one too many fear-mongering news stories about how the whole world would fall apart if the "wrong person" won, I shared these words with my friends on social media:

> **Here is what I know:** Someone will be elected president tomorrow. That person will have serious flaws. That person will have legitimate character concerns. That person will serve for at least 1,460 days, whether we like them or not.
>
> **Here is what I also know:** That person will not keep us from sharing our spare bedroom with the person who is down on their luck. That person will not stop us from inviting the homeless guy on the corner to eat lunch with us. That person will not keep us from stopping to help the dog on the side of the road. That person cannot keep our brains from saying prayers or our hands from giving good gifts or our mouths from speaking kind words to our neighbors in need.

> In fact, it could be argued that our collective capacity to do good and love our neighbor has the potential to do more than any person in any position of power could ever do.

In the past few years, these truths have been reinforced in my life again and again. There are so many beautifully small, seemingly insignificant, non-newsworthy moments of kindness happening all around us every day. At first glance, they may seem unimportant. But the more we focus on them and add them up and combine them with other people's collections, the more powerful they grow.

So if you find yourself on the verge of despair, wondering if you can handle even one more heart-wrenching news story or ridiculous political statement, I'll share some of my favorite small but mighty moments of kindness with you:

### LITTLE MOMENT OF KINDNESS #1

One morning, I finished a long run around picturesque Town Lake in Austin, Texas. I passed hundreds of other people out walking and running on this gorgeous fall morning. But it was a homeless woman slumped against the outside of a building near my posh hotel who gave me the largest and most genuinely kind smile out of everyone surrounding me. *Lord, give me the grace to offer that kind of love to others. Lord, give me eyes to see the angels among us.*

### LITTLE MOMENT OF KINDNESS #2

My wife, Stacey, got a flat tire one day.
I went to change it for her.
Then my car jack bent. A lot.
I was sad.
Then mad.
Because I had a lot to do that day.
Then a college student named Andrew asked me if I needed help.
I said, "Nah, I'm good."
I was lying.
Andrew could tell.
He got his jack from his car and started helping me anyway.
It still took us an hour to get it done.
Andrew was kind and patient the whole time.
Andrew will be getting a very nice gift card in the mail.
*Thank you, Andrew.*

### LITTLE MOMENT OF KINDNESS #3

A friend called one day with no agenda other than to say, "I believe in you." It was such a gift to me.

Words matter. Words create worlds. Words build up or break apart. Words bless or destroy. Our words can either be weapons of mass destruction or instruments of peace. We choose. Conversation after conversation, email after email, post after post. Let us choose our words wisely and with kindness.

I'm going to keep collecting these stories and storing them up in my "sometimes weary for this world" heart. They remind me of the power in each of us to spread joy, share love, and give grace to each person we meet. They remind me not to underestimate how small moments of kindness can change the world, and not to overestimate how grand, newspaper-worthy moments actually change anything. They help me grow into the kind of person I want to be and create the kind of world I want to live in.

The more I look for these little moments of kindness, the more I see them. And the more I see them, the more I know that we're going to be alright.

# THE KINGDOM OF HEAVEN

It's hard to comprehend the upside-down nature of the Kingdom of Heaven. We have such a strong cultural pull toward the boldest, biggest, richest, tallest, most "beautiful" things in life. But over and over again, Jesus calls us to shift our priorities and learn to see the world with new eyes. It's one of my very favorite qualities of his.

There's a church near me that drops Easter eggs from a helicopter each year. It's a grand spectacle. People flock to it, newspapers write about it, the local news sends a crew out to film it, and of course, the kids all love it. I think it's a great analogy of how we wait for the Kingdom of Heaven to show up. We want something big, flashy, fun, and family-friendly, forgetting that Jesus was simple, subversive, and born in a stable. We're staring up, looking for the helicopter, and we walk right past the barn.

This isn't an attack on that church. Their outreach idea has likely drawn many new people to their church community. But it is a reminder of how easily we turn toward fancy displays of extravagance and away from small signs of God's presence. We seek the once-a-year thrill rather than the daily awareness of God in easily overlooked places.

And the saddest part is that as we wait for the grand moments of the Kingdom, we miss the actual Kingdom as it pokes its head around corners, tiptoes through the shadows, and lies waiting on the margins of society. We ignore or misunderstand or devalue the work of God all around us because we're waiting for something more exciting to happen.

I know this because I've lived this. For most of my life, I've not only been the one looking for the helicopter but also the one coming up with the whole idea in the first place. Heck, I've even been the helicopter a few times. I know how to draw a crowd. I know how to create a spectacle. I know how to rally support. But my focus on the bold, big, and beautiful has come at a cost. I've missed so much—so many opportunities to love and listen, so many chances to discover God in the people and places around me, so many moments of heaven here on earth.

The religious leaders of Jesus's time had the same struggle. They desperately wanted a king who showed up with power and authority and put everyone in their place. So of course they were deeply disturbed that Jesus would rather hang out with prostitutes than play up to their expectations. They were waiting for the helicopter to drop thousands of Easter eggs and totally missed the Kingdom of Heaven in their midst.

Jesus told us that the Kingdom of Heaven is actually like a mustard seed and a little yeast. Those seemingly small things that are unseen, ignored, overlooked, and just plain ordinary. Those things that will grow and manifest into something enormous and beneficial if given the space.

What if we woke up every day and really believed Jesus's upside-down message? Suddenly we'd be able to see God at work all around, in, and through us. And we would find the Kingdom of Heaven among us already. At my very, very best (which is less often than I care to admit), I believe and remember the following:

> The Kingdom of Heaven is like rejoicing in the fact that you are not broken.
>
> The Kingdom of Heaven is like believing that you are extraordinary.
>
> The Kingdom of Heaven is like crawling into the lap of God and feeling Her delight.
>
> The Kingdom of Heaven is like learning to love and accept both sides and all parts of yourself.
>
> The Kingdom of Heaven is like celebrating everyone's superpowers.
>
> The Kingdom of Heaven is like friends you can be real and vulnerable with.
>
> The Kingdom of Heaven is like realizing you are worthy of being known.
>
> The Kingdom of Heaven is like becoming Real.
>
> The Kingdom of Heaven is like receiving the genuine love of someone who expects nothing in return.

The Kingdom of Heaven is like enjoying little sparks of generosity.

The Kingdom of Heaven is like appreciating where you are today.

The Kingdom of Heaven is like being fully present, fully aware, and fully open to connecting with others.

The Kingdom of Heaven is like countless little moments of kindness.

The Kingdom of Heaven is being ushered in and happening all around us but almost never in the ways we expect. Maybe that's actually the whole point.

# FINAL THOUGHTS ON MEANING MAKING

You might have noticed that the title, *Meaning Making*, never appeared in this book until now. That's not an accident. From the outset, the intent of this book was to give you the space you needed to go on your own journey of meaning making. That wouldn't be done with integrity if I was forcefully instructing you along the way.

Meaning making is a personal journey, and it's not a fast or an easy one. In a culture that values quick fixes and top-ten lists and skimmable content, meaning making can cause deep discomfort. While everyone else is racing by, the meaning maker chooses to pause. Purposely. While everyone else is searching for the next big thing, the meaning maker cultivates gratitude for each small gift. Regularly.

Meaning making is deeply necessary, but it doesn't happen without focus and intention. I've gotten halfway through life and built an impressive résumé with accomplishments and accolades lined up behind my name. But in all those years, I never learned to meaning make. I've done plenty of making to be sure, but I've mostly lacked the discipline and intentionality to attach meaning to much of these last forty years.

As driven, hungry, and compelled as I am to live a life of deep purpose, I also refuse to keep pushing forward at this pace. I am terrified to double the number of years I've lived on this earth or double the length of my résumé without ever having learned to meaning make along the way.

So I titled this book *Meaning Making* like I was offering up a prayer about what I yearn for in the next half of life. Writing this book forced me to meaning make regularly over many months. These pages are the culmination of trying to make sense of the life I've lived but have not always experienced along the way. I hope something in my messy learning has prompted deeper reflection for you, too. But more than that, I hope this book is the starting line for both of us to commit to meaning make more, better, and more intentionally throughout the rest of our lives.

Standing somewhere near this statistical halfway point in life reminds me of how I felt when I first arrived in Ghana. I had traveled a long way and was eager to tackle all of the work in front of me. When I got to one of the first remote fishing villages on our journey, I was told to wait under the mango tree. I grew restless and sweaty and frustrated as I waited. And waited. But while I waited, the entire village slowly joined me in the shade.

When everyone had finally arrived, the Chief turned to me and said in his native tongue, "Where have you been and where are you going?" I paused. That wasn't what I had expected. As I stumbled through my answer, I realized his deep wisdom. Reflecting on the past and setting intentions for the future illuminates the present.

This book is a marker in my own journey of those two questions. It's an opportunity for me to remember where I've been.

It has also clarified where I want to go and how I want to think differently. That's the essence of meaning making. We reflect on good moments so that we remember them deeply and don't blow past them. And we reflect on the not-so-good moments, trusting that we'll discover some deeper understanding about life so that the pain is not wasted. These reflections help us walk into the future with greater gratitude and wisdom.

In this book, I have reflected on a smattering of random, unsensational stories from my own life and ultimately landed in a place of great meaning. I hope that inspires you to go on a similar journey. Your path won't look the same as mine. That's why I haven't given you a guidebook or a road map or ten simple steps to meaning making. Instead, I wanted to create a sacred space of reflection where you could draw your own conclusions, create your own map, make your own meaning, and write your own stories.

In stark contrast to my other books, this one doesn't end with any detailed prescriptions. There are times when your doctor gives you medicine with very clear instructions on when and how to take it. Then there are times when your doctor just says you need more sunshine and exercise. This is my version of the latter. The only thing I really want you to do is truly know and believe down deep in your soul that you are not broken. You are worthy of being known. And, if you look closely enough, you will find that the world is filled with beautiful messes. I feel so very sure of that. Here's to more meaning making, my friend. For all of us.

# ABOUT THE AUTHOR

Chris Field is an award-winning author and two-time TEDx speaker. He is the founder of Mercy Project, an innovative nonprofit that combats child trafficking in Ghana's fishing industry. Mercy Project has rescued, rehabilitated, and reintegrated nearly three hundred formerly enslaved children back into their families.

Chris has broken multiple Guinness world records, run dozens of marathons, and taught hundreds of business students at Texas A&M University. His previous books include *Disrupting for Good* and *A Billion Hours of Good*. He lives in College Station, Texas, with his wife, Stacey, and their four children.

While all of this sounds really important and impressive (which he understands is the point of this section), he's also just a regular guy who loses his temper, forgets his wallet, messes up a lot, and has a whole host of shortcomings equally as unimpressive as the two paragraphs above. In other words, he's a beggar on a journey for bread, just like everyone else in the world.

More from Chris Field

*Disrupting for Good*
*A Billion Hours of Good*

Available today on Amazon.